*"Write down the revelation
and make it plain on tablets
so that a herald may run with it.
For the revelation awaits an appointed time;
it speaks of the end
and will not prove false.
Though it linger, wait for it;
it will certainly come
and will not delay."*

(Habakkuk 2:1-3)

*"If the watchman sees the sword coming against the land
and blows the trumpet to warn the people, then if anyone
hears the trumpet but does not take warning and the
sword comes and takes his life, his blood will be on his
own head. If he had taken warning, he would have saved
himself. But if the watchman sees the sword coming and
does not blow the trumpet to warn the people and the
sword comes and takes the life of one of them, that man
will be taken away because of his sin, but I will hold the
watchman accountable for his blood."*

(Ezekiel 33:3-6)

The Two Israels of God
in the Last Days

The Two Israels of God
in the Last Days

Richard David Thompson

New Wine Press

New Wine Press
An imprint of
Roperpenberthy Publishing Ltd
Springfield House
23 Oatlands Drive
Weybridge KY13 9LZ
United Kingdom

ISBN 978-1-905991-78-5

Typeset by **documen**, www.documen.co.uk
Printed in the United Kingdom

CONTENTS

Introduction

The Jews are a truly remarkable people due entirely to their indescribably gracious and merciful God. Because of Israel's unique calling, Satan has singled her out for extra hatred and vilification, far more so than any other nation. Certainly the Jews are a long way from perfect but many media reports about them have been very biased, incorrect and sometimes blatantly untrue due to these spiritual forces at work. Also today, the spirit of anti-Semitism is not just limited to Europe – it is growing throughout the whole earth.

The world is entirely blind to the spiritual forces, hence the confusion regarding the Jews' return to the land of Israel. Unfortunately, there is also much ignorance in a large part of the Church due to a misinterpretation of several scriptures, which has given rise to two main views – Replacement Theology and the Pro-Israel standpoint. There are a wide range of misunderstandings on both sides of the debate which I will seek to address. On the Replacement side there are many scriptures which are ignored. The Pro-Israel side have numerous beliefs on certain issues relating to the Old Covenant which, in the light of the New Covenant, are not now biblically correct for born again believers, whether Jew or

Gentile. These include ideas that in the End-Times, God will be involved in the rebuilding of the stone temple in Jerusalem with its sacrificial system. This will actually be instigated by the Antichrist who will lead most of the Jews even further astray than they are today. Another misunderstanding is that Messianic Jews should continue to observe the special days of the Old Covenant, but this is contrary to teaching in the New Testament. Paul fervently taught both Jews and Gentiles alike that in Christ they were free from the law:

> *"But now that you know God—or rather are known by God—how is it that you are turning back to those weak and miserable forces* (of the law)? *Do you wish to be enslaved by them all over again? You are observing special days and months and seasons and years! I fear for you, that somehow I have wasted my efforts on you."*
>
> (Galatians 4:9-11)

He did make an important proviso in Romans 14:1-23, that if a man considers one day more sacred than another he should not be judged. However, he qualified this teaching by saying in verse 1 that the individual was weak in faith, whereas God wants us to mature and become strong in our believing.

As an ex-Pharisee of the Pharisees, Paul knew that although the Messianic Jews could accept that Jesus fulfilled the law in its entirety, the implications of this for them would be extremely controversial and far reaching. It had taken the dramatic intervention of God on the road to Damascus and three years in the wilderness to turn this fiery zealot around to accurately understand and teach the New Covenant! So profound were these changes that, in his letter to the believers in Rome, Paul deliberately and carefully explained the doctrine of the Christian faith regarding Israel. There were a significant number of Messianic Jews in the church there who knew the law, Rom. 7:1, and so he comprehensively clarified Israel's standing before God, both before and after Christ. For instance, in Romans 11 he wrote:

> *"I ask then: Did God reject his people? By no means! I am an Israelite myself, a descendant of Abraham, from the tribe of Benjamin. God did not reject his people, whom he foreknew."*
>
> (Verses 1-2)

> *"Again I ask: Did they stumble so as to fall beyond recovery? Not at all! Rather, because of their transgression, salvation has come to the Gentiles to make Israel envious* (Gk. parazelos). *But if their transgression means riches for the world, and their loss means riches for the Gentiles, how much greater riches will their fullness bring!"*
>
> (Verses 11-12)

The original Greek word *"parazelos"* literally means "jealous" rather than "envious" as is translated in the NIV. Envy is a strong desire for something which is not ours to have, whereas jealousy is an equally strong feeling for something that is ours by right.

> *"And so all Israel* (the surviving remnant before Jesus returns) *will be saved"*

"As far as the gospel is concerned, they (the Jews)
are enemies for your (the Gentiles') *sake; but as far as
election is concerned, they are loved on account of the
patriarchs, for God's gifts and his call are irrevocable.
Just as you who were at one time disobedient to God have
now received mercy as a result of their disobedience,
so they too have become disobedient in order that **they
too may now receive mercy as a result of God's mercy
to you***"

(Verse 28-31)

Paul is saying in these last verses that God used the Jews'
disobedience to bring mercy to the Gentiles. Their rejection
of Jesus resulted in Him being handed over to the Romans
for execution. Unbeknown to them, they were helping to
bring about the fulfilment of all their feasts as Jesus became
the sacrifice that all the rituals had pictured. He took the
punishment not only for their sins but for those of the whole
world. What mercy and grace! Through faith in Christ the
Jews no longer have to perform the feasts to keep themselves
acceptable before our holy Creator God. His will is now for
Gentile believers who have received His mercy to live in the
good of it and to show this same mercy to the Jews. As we
Gentiles grow in receiving and ministering God's love to
them, they will become jealous and desire it for themselves.
This will draw the Jews to Christ that they might be saved.
Shamefully, Christendom has shown them the exact opposite
over the centuries.

Before starting the first chapter, I would like to share
two visions that the Lord graciously gave me whilst
visiting Jerusalem back in 1977, which are highly relevant

to this study. The Lord had told me to go to Israel and I duly went that year. The first vision, given through a minister on the Christian tour, was of me standing on the walls of Jerusalem. The Lord said, "look out and see what is approaching the city and warn the people about what you see. I am making you a watchman of My word". The second one regarding the nation of Israel was given to me directly. I saw two long lines that crossed each other, similar to a multiplication sign but flattened and elongated. The Lord revealed to my spirit that the long line from top left gradually sloping downwards to bottom right represented His righteous judgments on the nation of Israel coming to an end. The long line gradually ascending from bottom left to top right was His merciful restoration increasing on her. Since my conversion I have always been an avid student of the Bible, and God has shown me more clearly what He was meaning in both visions.

This study is in response to these and other words given to me over the years. It is also a sequel to my book Almost Midnight, which provides further teaching about God's dealings with Israel and the Church before the momentous and glorious return of the Lord Jesus Christ. The issues dealt with in both books will become more and more important as we approach and go through the Great End-Time Tribulation. Understanding these scriptures will greatly aid our outreach and discipling of new believers. The Church will be able to explain from the Bible not only about the wonderful salvation we have in Christ and how to walk in it, but the spiritual significance of world events in the Middle East and Europe, and where we are in God's End-time plans. I trust this study will help move us towards that goal.

1 The Two Israels

As mentioned, there is an extremely wide spectrum of thinking in the Church about Israel but understanding that the Bible refers to her in two different ways will help to unravel the subject. Confusion between these definitions has in part contributed to the two main doctrinal viewpoints mentioned in the Introduction, namely Replacement Theology and the Pro-Israel view. The former is a belief system held by those who think Israel has been totally replaced by the Church because Jesus fulfilled the Old Covenant in its entirety and brought in the New Covenant through His shed blood, death and resurrection, that Israel has been cut off as a nation and the promises to her have all been invested in the Church. The Israelites, therefore, have no territorial claim to their historic land and it is not God who brought about the restoration of the Jewish State in 1948. The Pro-Israel view is held by those who believe the Jews still retain special status before God along with a divine right to the land because of the covenant He made with Abraham and his descendants. Some in the former group now tend to refer to their viewpoint as Fulfilment Theology. It is important to say there are correct points on both sides.

A proper biblical understanding regarding Israel's position before God today is therefore essential, as there are very serious spiritual and political implications to her presence in the Middle East. So let me define the two Israels of God as found in the Bible. Firstly, all Jewish people, whether their beliefs are scripturally correct or not, i.e. Messianic, atheistic or whatever, are collectively part of the nation of Israel. They are considered by the Bible as descendants of Abraham and remain a special people called by God to be set apart from all other nations because the *"gifts and calling of God are irrevocable"*, *Rom. 11:29*. The second Israel describes both Jews and **Gentiles** who have truly believed and obeyed God's Word in their hearts, not just since the New Covenant came into being but stretching way back to Abraham. Paul specifically describes these true believers as *"the Israel of God"*, *Gal. 6:16*. So all Jews are called to be a special people but the second group are those Jews who have personally responded to God's calling. It is to this latter group that believing Gentiles are joined. Gentile believers become fellow citizens with the true Jewish believers, as only faith in Jesus is acceptable to God for both Jew and Gentile, Ephes.2:12. The writer to the Hebrews confirms this by saying *"But you have come to Mount Zion, to the heavenly Jerusalem, the city of the living God"*, Heb. 12:22. Any Jews living outside Israel fall into these two categories as well.

These two groups are clearly recognised by Paul, as seen when he wrote to the Church in Rome.

*"For I could wish that I myself were cursed and cut off from Christ for the sake of my people, those of my own race, **the people of Israel**. Theirs is the adoption; theirs*

the divine glory, the covenants, the receiving of the law,
the temple worship and the promises. Theirs are the
patriarchs, and from them is traced the human ancestry of
the Messiah, who is God over all, forever praised! Amen.
*It is not as though God's word had failed. For **not all who***
are descended from Israel are Israel."

(Romans 9:3-6)

It is vital to see from both the Old and New Testaments that only those who have sincerely accepted God's Word and trusted it are saved. Before the covenant was made with Abraham, everything was much simpler but faith was still essential. For instance, Abel offered a better sacrifice than Cain and was reckoned as a righteous man because he walked by faith and was therefore saved, Heb. 11:4. Cain's sacrifice was not acceptable. Paul again highlighted this difference between believing and unbelieving Jews when he wrote that certain Jews had fallen short of God's requirements.

"But the people of Israel, who pursued the law as the way
of righteousness, have not attained their goal. Why not?
Because they pursued it not by faith but as if it were by
works. They stumbled over the "stumbling stone.""

(Romans 9:31-32)

In their own understanding of living in righteousness, many had tried to obey the law through their own efforts rather than walking humbly before God by faith in His Word. They had remained unbelievers in God's eyes. Paul taught that faith comes when God speaks into our hearts, *"faith comes from hearing, and hearing through the word of God"*, Rom. 10:17.

We can then respond to Him by using the faith that has been given through the revealed Word. It is through this gift of faith that we receive God's righteousness and come into relationship with Him, Rom. 3:22.

Unbelieving Jews included all those who had the outward appearance of faithfulness but were effectively just paying "lip service" to God regarding Judaism. Jesus described them as *"whitewashed tombs"*, Matt. 23:27. They looked good on the outside but inside they had death and darkness. They were not changed in their hearts because they did not actually believe and receive God's promises and instructions as given through Abraham and Moses. Although they were zealous in quoting the scriptures and attempting to live by them, they denied themselves salvation because of unbelief. This dire spiritual situation in Israel became vividly exposed by John the Baptist and Jesus when they ministered to the Jews in their day. It is very similar to nominal Christians in the Church age who "go to church", say the right words and sing the right songs but only have a natural understanding of the truth. They have not opened up their hearts sufficiently to receive revelation from the Spirit about the good news of Jesus Christ, and the accompanying faith to believe it. Consequently, there is no new birth. This is the difference between a nominal and born again believer.

It is also very important to say that salvation under the Abrahamic Covenant was not exclusive to Jews alone. Although they were forbidden to marry foreigners who did not worship and love Yahweh as their God, they could marry and include as many foreigners as would accept and walk in His ways. Consequently, as Gentiles recognized the truths in the Old Testament many people from other nations put their

faith in Yahweh and became true believers, for instance, the
many Egyptians who left with Moses at the Exodus.

"Many other people went up with them (into the
wilderness), *and also large droves of livestock, both flocks
and herds."*

(Exodus 12:38)

Ruth, the Moabitess, is a classic example of a Gentile
becoming a Jewess and what's more, she gave birth to a son
who was the grandfather of King David, Ruth 4:17.

Many nationalities from the Persian Empire also converted
to Judaism after seeing God's awesome power at work in
delivering the Jews from Haman's evil plot to kill them all.

*"... and many people of other nationalities became Jews
because fear of the Jews had seized them."*

(Esther 8:17)

The Psalmist also wrote of this multiplicity of people believing
in the Lord.

*"He has founded his city on the holy mountain. The
LORD loves the gates of Zion more than all the other
dwellings of Jacob. Glorious things are said of you,
city of God: "I will record Rahab and Babylon among
those who acknowledge me — Philistia too, and Tyre,
along with Cush — and will say, 'This one was born in
Zion.'" Indeed, of Zion it will be said, "This one and
that one were born in her, and the Most High himself will
establish her." The LORD will write in the register of the*

peoples:"This one was born in Zion." As they make music
they will sing, "All my fountains are in you."

(Psalm 87:1-7)

(Here and in future quotes, where LORD is shown in capitals it refers to the divine name of God, which is YHWH (Yahweh) meaning I am that I am, the anglicised form being Jehovah).

It is clear that those who accepted the God of the Jews and who followed Him became Israelites. It was the duty of all Jews to be a light to the Gentiles, Isaiah 42:6, so the latter could be saved by turning from their idols to worshipping Yahweh. The Jews clearly failed, for the most part, in this calling as before Christ it was the only way to be saved. God's salvation has always been truly universal for all who believe His Word and was definitely not exclusive to the genetic sons of Abraham through Isaac and Jacob.

From observation today, it is apparent that the majority of Jewish people are a mix of unbelieving atheistic Jews, practising Jews and Jews with all manner of different beliefs. Consequently, they all remain unsaved. There are only a small percentage who are true spiritual Jews in the heart and they are the ones who have put their trust in Jesus Christ. Many of them prefer to be called Messianic Jews, rather than Christians, in keeping with the Hebrew language. They have genuinely sought God and the Holy Spirit has been able to reveal Jesus to them.

Indeed, this is what happened to Saul of Tarsus. It was through sincere zealousness for the truth, as he understood it, that he persecuted the Church but God was able to harness his genuine motive to good effect. Although he consented to the death of Stephen, he had heard him preach the gospel,

Acts 7:1- 8:1, and God used this to pierce his heart. As a matter of interest, Paul was his Roman name, not a new God given Christian one. He was an apostle to the Gentiles and this name became accepted over the course of time.

Jesus said to the practising Jews of His day:

> *"If you believed Moses, you would believe me, for he wrote about me. But since you do not believe what he wrote, how are you going to believe what I say?"*
>
> (John 5:46-47)

> *"Everyone who listens to the Father and learns from him comes to me."*
>
> (John 6:45)

These unbelievers are a part of the first definition of Israel.

Replacement Theology does not accept that the nation of Israel, whether believing or unbelieving, continues as a special people before God. However, this contradicts God's promises to them such as the one spoken by Jeremiah just prior to the Jews' exile into Babylon:

> *"This is what the Lord says, he appoints the sun to shine by day, who decrees the moon and stars by night, who stirs up the sea so that its waves roar – the Lord Almighty is his name: "If this fixed order departs from me," declares the Lord, "then the offspring of Israel also will cease from being a nation before Me forever.""*
>
> (Jeremiah 31:35-37)

Therefore, since the sun, moon and stars are still shining, all Jews remain a special people before Him. The only practical condition that God put on them through the Abrahamic Covenant was circumcision and this is still required today for those Jews who reject their Messiah Jesus.

"Any uncircumcised male, who has not been circumcised in the flesh, will be cut off from his people; he has broken my covenant."

(Genesis 17:14)

This physical ritual was, and still is, an essential part of the Abrahamic covenant for the Jew who has not yet received Christ, Gen.17:1-14. It points to the work of the Holy Spirit who crucifies us with Jesus at conversion, giving us a new clean heart and enabling the Spirit to permanently indwell us, Ezek. 36:26-27. Accordingly, if Messianic Jews have not been circumcised, there is no need for them to do so. However, for a Jew who rejects Jesus and the cross, the requirement given to Abraham still stands. Unsaved Jews can rightly claim the land under this covenant, but they must also accept circumcision, along with the law.

The current ingathering of Jews to Israel from the four corners of the earth is based on God's faithfulness to His word to them, not on their faithfulness to Him. As already quoted, Paul's teaching in Romans about these promises to the Jewish nation says *"God's gifts and calling are irrevocable"*, *Rom. 11:29*, i.e. nothing can change them. Thankfully, we serve a Creator who is perfect, faithful and never fails on the greatest or even the least of His promises.

Believing that the Jews no longer have any right to the land has led some to say that setting up the State of Israel was a political mistake causing unnecessary problems. Unfortunately, some of Replacement persuasion with the best of intentions are siding with the likes of Hamas in Gaza but it is a misguided and unscriptural quest to appease the Muslims. It will not bring peace as I will explain in the next chapter. Others, looking at the situation naturally, liken the conflict to the "troubles" in Northern Ireland where big strides forward have been made in resolving their issues. However, the Israeli/Palestinian impasse is a much deeper and far more sinister problem, hence we must understand what the scriptures actually say about these matters.

All the murderous attempts over the centuries to exterminate and scatter the Jews have not stopped them finally returning to their land today and prospering in a truly miraculous way. This is in spite of the majority stubbornly rejecting their Messiah and being involved with a multitude of false religions, many even denying Yahweh's existence. But why is there so much intense hatred towards Israel, particularly from the Muslim nations? Why is this return happening and why in our day? We will consider the answers to the last two questions in subsequent chapters, so let first us look at the reasons for Muslim opposition.

2 The Reasons Why Islam is Against the Jews

For those who do not understand the Bible or the Koran with regard to Israel, it is impossible to see the real intentions behind the spirit of Islam, and one might even think a Two State Solution is the only possible, sensible and just way to achieve peace. Although it is not currently politically correct to question this, it is both contrary to God's covenant with Abraham and unthinkable from a fundamental Islamic viewpoint.

The angel that spoke to Muhammad called itself Gabriel, but he mistakenly believed it was the Holy Spirit speaking to him. It was neither because it taught things so totally opposed to the scriptures in the Old and New Testaments. Consequently, it is obvious that the Muslim Allah is not the God of the Bible. In 610 AD, as instructed by this spirit, Muhammad began to preach that not only were all the 360 or so gods being worshipped in Mecca false, but the Jews had made changes to the Old Testament during their exile in Babylon. Likewise, the disciples had purposely not written down the correct version of Jesus' teachings and life on the earth. The Koran frequently refers to these supposed fraudulent changes, e.g. Suras 2:75 and 5:13-14 (Sura being a chapter in the Koran). The spirit said that the Old and New Testaments had been so perverted by the Jews and Christians respectively, that anyone believing them could not be saved from hell as the words are not what Allah originally taught.

It also said to Muhammad that Abraham, Ishmael, Isaac, Jacob, Moses and Jesus were all Allah's prophets and that they, along with a limited number of others, were the only Jews who had been obedient to Allah, Sura 2:136. Although Muhammad considered Jesus to be a prophet, his writings in the Koran do not include the majority of Jesus' teachings such as forgiving, loving and praying for one's enemies etc. They also deny Jesus' divinity and teach that Judas heroically died in His place on the cross. This is why Muslims believe Jesus was able to appear to the disciples for 40 days after His supposed resurrection – because He was never crucified. All this absolutely contradicts the Christian and Jewish faiths, the former having been accepted for nearly 600 years before Islam was birthed and the latter some 1,500 years before that.

Islamic sources say that Muhammad originally did not believe it was God who spoke to him but a false spirit. However, after much encouragement from one of his several wives, he persevered with these traumatic visitations and started to believe God was talking to him through Gabriel. One of his wives was a twelve year old girl, although some accounts say she was even younger.

Muhammad believed he had the real truth and was the last great prophet promised by Almighty God. However, Moses had actually said in the Bible that the great prophet who was to come after him would be from the Israelites and all must listen and obey Him or be called to account before God:

"The LORD said to me (Moses)*: "What they say is good. I will raise up for them a prophet like you from among their fellow Israelites, and I will put my words in his mouth. He will tell them everything I command him. I myself will call to account anyone who does not listen to my words that the prophet speaks in my name.*

(Deuteronomy 18:17-19)

This prophet is referring to Jesus who clearly came from the Israelites and was also prophesied to come from the royal line of King David. Islam declares that Muhammad was the fulfilment of the above scripture but ignores the necessity of the prophet being a Jew, coming from the royal lineage and numerous other essential requirements foretold elsewhere in the Old Testament.

The Bible beautifully demonstrates that God is love and desires to relate to His creation. In contrast, the Koran reveals the Islamic Allah to be a remote and distant spirit, not wanting a relationship with man, only submission and worship from him. There is also no concept in the Koran that God is absolutely holy and requires every sin to be punished, not just forgiven. Consequently, in their view there was no need for Jesus to die for the sins of the world. All this is diametrically opposite to both Old and New Testaments which clearly show that God required a sacrifice for the sins of the whole world and that Jesus, God's son, went to the cross for all mankind. This fulfilled countless Old Testament prophecies but there is nothing prophesied in the Bible about Muhammad.

Although Muhammad was greatly confused regarding what the Old and New Testaments actually said and meant, certain parts of the Koran are clearly taken from the Old Testament but in a very distorted and limited way. The spirit agreed with the Bible in saying that the sons of Israel were the Chosen People, Moses delivered them from Egypt, they were given the Law, spent forty years in the wilderness, possessed the Promised Land and had prophets such as David and Jesus who lived in Jerusalem etc, Suras 2:47-92, 5:20-26 and 17:104. But the truth was twisted when it said that the Jewish prophets were all obedient Muslims who were following Allah. Below are two of the many verses from the Koran which agree with the Bible:

"O Children of Israel! Remember My favour that I bestowed upon you and how I preferred you above all the worlds".

(Sura 2:47)

"And (remember) *when we made a covenant with you, and raised the Mount* (the law given at Sinai) *above you, saying, "Hold fast to what We have given you."*

(Sura 2:93)

Islam says that Muhammad was sent to expose the major errors of doctrine and to teach the Jews what Allah had really said in the first place. Muslims see that the burning of Jerusalem, the destruction of the Temple in 70 AD, and the exile were confirmation that Allah was punishing the Jews for all their gross sins and errors.

In 135 AD, over 400 years before Muhammad was even born, an attempt was made by the Roman Emperor Hadrian (of wall building fame) to remove all evidence that the Jews had ever lived in the land. After Titus had destroyed Jerusalem and the Temple in 70 AD, Hadrian ploughed up the city and completely rebuilt it for his soldiers. He changed the name of Israel to Palestine after the Philistines, who were one of the people groups living there before the Jews. He constructed a much enlarged plinth on King Solomon's temple site and built a hexagonal place of worship on it, dedicated to three of the main Roman gods – Jupiter, Juno and Minerva. He also changed the name of Jerusalem to Aelia Capitolina Triad. This was a combination of his clan name Aelia, and Capitolina Triad which referred to three major gods, chief of whom was Jupiter.

Around 312 AD, the Roman Emperor Constantine accepted Christianity and in 320 AD he made Jerusalem a place of pilgrimage by building the Church of the Holy Sepulchre on the site where he believed the crucifixion and burial of Jesus had taken place. At the same time he destroyed the Roman temple and rebuilt a church on the Temple site, octagonal in shape, similar to the central shape of the Church of the Nativity he constructed in Bethlehem. It seems that the Muslims may have thought that the ruins of this one were the foundations of Solomon's temple, and in their desire to replicate it, as they believe Solomon was a Muslim prophet of Allah, it was constructed in the octagonal shape, which is highly unusual for a Muslim building.

In 610 AD, Muhammad started to spread his new religion in Mecca by speaking against the gods of Arabia, but in 622 AD he was "railroaded" out of the city by the Arabs for his preaching. He retreated to Medina where he made converts by peaceful means, saying it was their freewill choice whether to believe in his Islamic Allah or not. He wrote Sura 2:250 which says that "There is no compulsion in religion". This is the verse that many Muslims use to try and prove Islam is a peaceful religion. However, in 625 AD the spirit instructed Muhammad to use the scimitar in Jihad to eliminate those who refused to believe. This resulted in the Jewish population of Medina being slaughtered due to their rejection of his new religion. He said this latter teaching superseded the initial peaceful one, which means that the militant fundamentalists today are actually the true followers of Muhammad, because they obey his later instructions. Many liberal Muslims have altered the meaning of Jihad to be a fight against injustice etc. but it is not what Muhammad taught.

With this new teaching on Jihad, the Muslim armies speedily conquered Mecca and the remainder of what is now Saudi Arabia, before moving on to the rest of the Middle East. Allah took advantage of the vacuum left following the decline of the eastern half of the Roman Empire (Byzantine). Muhammad destroyed all shrines in Mecca except the cube shaped one where Hubal, the moon god, the chief spirit in the area, resided. He had demanded that his followers walk around the cube in an anticlockwise direction, bow down and pray towards it, and this is exactly what Allah demands today of Muslims. Although the statue of Hubal which stood in the shrine was broken to pieces, the building is said to have been purified by Muhammad. I believe the spirit which spoke to him was Hubal, and that this moon god and the Muslim Allah are one and the same spirit. It appeared to Muhammad as the angel Gabriel and continues to live in the shrine, now called the Ka'aba (meaning cube), which is draped in black and has the huge white mosque built around it. Significantly, the Holy of Holies in the Jewish temple was also a cube, 1 Kings 6:20, showing that the spirits imitate God where they can. A further telltale sign that Allah and Hubal are the same spirit is the new moon emblem on mosques and the flags of many Islamic countries.

In 622 AD when Muhammad arrived in Medina, 200 miles north of Mecca, he had had no instruction on which way to pray. Swayed by the large Jewish community living there and because he thought he was a true Jew, he chose to pray along with them towards Jerusalem, which was at least 500 miles further north of Medina. At that time Palestine was part of southern Syria, so Muhammad described the direction for prayer in terms familiar to the people in Arabia by stipulating that they should pray towards Syria. However, around 17 months after Muhammad had come to Medina, the spirit instructed him to pray towards the Ka'aba, which was in the opposite direction. The Koran says Abraham went down to Mecca in Arabia with Ishmael and rebuilt the Ka'aba, originally constructed by Adam. They reckon it was buried in the flood but Allah showed them where to look. It was dug up and consecrated to Allah along with the city which became the central place of worship for Muslims, Sura 2:125-127. By pointing Muhammad away from Jerusalem and southwards towards Mecca, Allah was saying that Mecca was the holiest place rather than Jerusalem. Again, this is completely contrary to God's Word.

After Muhammad's death, the Muslim Arab armies invaded Jerusalem in 638 AD and occupied it, ruling over the Jews as well as the Christians who were living and visiting there. With deliberate provocation towards the Jews, they erected a wooden structure on the Temple

Mount to demonstrate that their god was greater than the Jewish God, just as Hadrian had done before. The site had originally been called Mount Moriah back in Abraham's day, where in 2000 BC he went to sacrifice his son Isaac. The Jewish temple was built on this site by King Solomon 1,000 years later, 2 Chron.3:1. Muhammad did not actually say in the Koran that Ishmael was to be sacrificed, only that it was Abraham's son, Sura 37:102. It was not until after the prophet's death that the thought of it being Ishmael arose. Muhammad was from the Quraysh tribe, which was descended from Ishmael, and so believing that it was he, rather than Isaac, who Abraham was to sacrifice, it raised Muhammad to even greater importance.

Another point worth considering is to do with the Farthest Mosque. To Muslims, a mosque means a place of prayer. Just before Muhammad was hounded out of Mecca in 622 AD he had a night vision, which became known as the Night Journey. In the dream, he rode on a white winged horse with a woman's head and a peacock's tail to what he described as "the farthest mosque" where he prayed with Abraham and other deceased prophets, Sura 17:1. There was no indication from Muhammad that this referred to anywhere on earth, so it would seem, without any contrary evidence, that Muhammad was visiting heaven, which he described as the Farthest Mosque. As there were no mosques outside Arabia then and he had never even left the peninsula up to that point, this is even more likely to be the case.

The well respected Muslim historian and geographer, al Waqidi, states in his book Kitab al Magghazi that, at the time, there were only two places of prayer in Arabia visited by Muhammad where mosques had been built. He concludes that in earthly terms, the vision would have referred to the farthest one of these two from Mecca.

A new interpretation as to where the mosque might be situated emerged around the time of a rebellion against the Ummyyad Caliph Abdul Malik, whose seat of power was Damascus in Syria to the far north of Medina. The Ummyyad's form of Islamic rule was deemed too secular for many Muslims, so al Zubayr was made a rival Caliph and he headed up the revolt. He took control of Arabia which included Medina and Mecca, as well as various other areas such as modern day Iraq. He also stopped pilgrims in Syria who supported Malik from visiting the Ka'aba in Mecca. It was during this time, in about 690 AD, that Jerusalem was gaining acceptance as the new location of the Farthest Mosque.

Malik prevailed and eventually overcame the rebellion. He wanted a building to compete with the Holy Sepulchre, the Roman Catholic Church in Jerusalem, so he upgraded the wooden building over the rock on the Temple site. This had originally been erected by Omar, the third Caliph, to mark the Muslim conquest of the city in 638 AD. Malik also wanted to establish the new understanding that it was Ishmael who was involved in Abraham's test and not Isaac. He rebuilt the structure into the impressive Dome of the Rock shrine we see today. In 705 AD, Malik's son followed in his footsteps and built another mosque on the Temple Site to the south of the Dome, calling it the al Aqsa Mosque, meaning the Farthest Mosque, to commemorate the Night Journey to Jerusalem. This new location was then considered to be the place of prayer that Muhammad had gone to and is now accepted by Muslims worldwide as the correct one.

I emphasise that both these new interpretations came after Muhammad's death. Firstly, he had had the dream just before he fled to Medina in 622 AD when there were no mosques in Jerusalem, so the "farthest mosque" could not have referred to one there. If it was a prophetic dream of something in the future, he would have clearly explained this highly important location. And secondly, there is no mention in the Koran that Ishmael was the son who Abraham went to sacrifice.

Also, there is nothing from Muhammad to say that Allah had any intention of giving Muslims the Promised Land and so the only links they have with Jerusalem come from these two teachings that developed years after Muhammad's death in 632 AD. Eminent Muslim scholars say that there is no evidence in Islamic classical sources that Muhammad placed any importance on Jerusalem or the land. Indeed, the city is never mentioned once by name in the Koran, only that he prayed with the Jews towards Syria, before being directed to the Ka'aba. Over the centuries after the Koran and the original Hadiths were written, various other doctrines regarding Jerusalem developed but as they are not derived from the teachings of Muhammad, their last prophet, they are not strictly Islamic.

So why has this linkage between Islam and Jerusalem arisen and become so important, even to the point of Muslims being prepared to lay down their lives to control Israel and its capital? It is all to do with the promises God made to the Jewish nation that they would be restored to the land in the last days of this age. Unlike God, the Muslim Allah has no foreknowledge and one can only conclude that sometime after Muhammad died Allah realized that Jerusalem was still important to God and, in an effort to Islamise the city, came up with various teachings such as the Farthest Mosque being there and Abraham offering up Ishmael.

Since the fall of the Turkish Empire in 1917, various movements have emerged in Palestine which have been a mixture of Arab Nationalism and Islamic fervor, to try and overcome the Jewish claim to Jerusalem. Many of these Islamic ideas have also been accepted by those in the media and world governments who do not know the Bible, the actual history of Palestine or the spiritual battle that is raging over Jerusalem. All this extra Koranic teaching has led to a growing acceptance that the Temple site in Jerusalem and other holy Jewish sites, such as Abraham's tomb in Hebron, all belong to the Arabs rather than the Jews.

More recently, Christian Palestinian Liberation Theology has developed further thoughts which have even been adopted by some Palestinian Churches. They claim that Jesus, the prophets of Israel and other biblical characters were really Palestinians. Its teaching says that Arabs who lived in Palestine before 1917 were descended from the Jebusites and other tribes who were not killed by the Israelites. The Jebusites did indeed build Jerusalem before the Jews first conquered the land around 1500 BC but the link with present day Palestinians is entirely without historical or Biblical evidence. Also, the current Minister of the Interior in Gaza, Al Hekma, admitted on their T.V. channel in May 2012 that "Every Palestinian in Gaza and throughout Palestine can prove his Arab roots – half are from Egypt and the rest are from Jordan, Saudi Arabia, Yemen etc." He was trying to garner support from the surrounding Arab countries, not realizing he was actually undermining the Palestinian cause which is that they are mainly indigenous to Israel.

At the time of writing, the relatively moderate Arabs in the West Bank are led by President Mahmoud Abbas of Fatah, the ruling party there. Despite the numerous efforts of politicians from many countries, Fatah has still not removed the destruction of the State of Israel from their Charter, contradicting public statements to the U.N. that they have given up violence and have accepted the existence of Israel. It was President Nasser of Egypt who helped them form the Palestinian Liberation Organisation in 1964 with the sole objective of destroying the Jewish State. Just reclaiming the West Bank after the Israelis took it in 1967 has never been their prime objective, as Muslim Palestinians will never be satisfied with only half the land. Their true declared goal remains the annihilation of the Jews and their state.

Today, despite her brutal neighbours, Israel has agreed to a two-state solution but insists on the Palestinians recognizing the Jewish state. However, Fatah still cannot bring themselves to do this because it is contrary to their Charter which is based on the Islamic teaching just explained. They consider Palestine to be their territory and Jerusalem a Muslim capital. They say to the West that all they want is a state of their own in the West Bank, Gaza and the east part of Jerusalem (Old Jerusalem) and then there will be peace. But to their own people they speak, in Arabic, the real truth that they want the whole land. If they do achieve statehood, it will be a Trojan Horse, a stepping stone for them to increase their power base in order to eventually destroy the State of Israel.

Hamas, who govern the Gaza Strip in the south west, are an even more extreme Muslim group of Palestinians who have a catalogue of hatred towards the Jews actually written into their Charter. They claim to be mainly of Egyptian and

Saudi origin. When Hamas defeated Fatah at the elections in Gaza, they machine-gunned many of the Fatah Party workers and threw some from high buildings to their deaths, blindfolded with hands tied behind their backs, because they had been negotiating with Jews. The following portion is in the Hamas charter:

> *"The Islamic Resistance Movement believes*
> *that the land of Palestine is an Islamic Waqf*
> (meaning an endowment in law dedicated to God
> which cannot be reversed)... *It is consecrated*
> *for future generations until Judgment Day.*
> *It, or any part of it, should not be given up....*
> *There is no solution to the Palestinian question*
> *except through Jihad. Initiatives, proposals and*
> *international conferences are all a waste of time*
> *and vain endeavours."*

Part of the 1988 Hamas Charter

Hamas demands a Muslim state based on Sharia law, not just in Gaza and the West Bank but in the whole of Israel, without a Jew in sight. So, not only is a two state solution contrary to God's Word, but it is also contrary to their faith which has been added to since Muhammad died. Their Charter continues by quoting an accepted Hadith teaching which says:

> *"The Day of Judgment will not come about until Muslims fight the Jews. When the Jew hides behind stones and trees, the stones and trees will say O Muslims, O Abdullah, there is a Jew behind me, come and kill him."*

This command requires Muslims to kill Jews in order that the judgment of all mankind by their Allah can be brought about. Hence their deep desire to murder as many Jews as possible. Dying in Jihad enables them to by-pass the Last Judgment for sin at the end of this age and go directly to Paradise, where the men have a choice of several virgins as their reward.

The fundamentalists have had an enormous galvanizing effect on the rest of the Muslim world by shaming them for compromising the teachings of Islam, in particular, by changing the meaning of Jihad and agreeing to negotiate with Jews regarding the land. To their credit, Hamas has been more honest and has publically declared their position, whereas Fatah are led by deceitful politicians. The current attempt at a Reconciliation Agreement between Fatah and Hamas is a farce as they hate each other, surpassed only by their hatred of the Jews. Neither side trusts the other and in many instances, as mentioned, they will even kill one another. They cannot possibly be trusted to have a state of their own.

The Palestinians say that peace talks have failed because the Jews continue to build in the West Bank. However, when the Israelis called their bluff and stopped construction for 10 months in response to this demand, the Palestinians made no effort to re-enter negotiations, let alone recognize Israel's right to exist and alter their charters. They continue to teach their schoolchildren to hate Jews saying that a good Jew is a dead one. The Koran describes Jews as "apes", Sura 2:65. Continuing to teach these things in their schools is contrary to the Oslo Accords which say both governments should stop propagating hatred. Fatah also calls for a total withdrawal of Israeli soldiers from the West Bank. However, when Israel pulled her troops out of Gaza and forcibly removed her own citizens in the hope of peace, all they received in return were rockets. Withdrawal from the West Bank would mean UN troops replacing the Israeli army, but from Israel's past experience of this type of thing, it doesn't bode well for peace. UN troops were stationed in southern Lebanon after the 34 day war in July 2006 to ensure that Hezbollah did not re-arm, but thanks to the U.N. turning a blind eye to arms shipments from Iran through Syria, the Shia Muslim militia there are better armed now than they were before the conflict.

Considering the larger picture, Islam is not just content with conquering Israel, it wants all of Europe, Africa, America, and then on to India and China – the whole world in fact. The imperialist objective revealed in the Koran is to conquer all peoples and impose Sharia law which will have a devastating effect on every person on this planet. Western and Eastern civilisations are being invaded and challenged. Islam is bullying Western leaders to concede to its demands, and the sooner the world wakes up to what is happening the better.

It must be understood that fundamental Islam is not only incompatible with Judaism but also with every religion and secular group in the world, as its objective is to convert and dominate. Remember the slaughter that occurred in India when around a million people were murdered during the formation of Pakistan because the Muslims refused to live side by side with Hindus. Muslim opposition to Christians in the Middle East and elsewhere is intense. Churches have been blown up in Egypt and many other places around the world. There has also been a dramatic reduction of Christians in Gaza and Bethlehem, some of whom were murdered. The list of areas where Christians are being killed or having to flee for their lives just increases with time, e.g. Northern Nigeria,

Northern Sudan, Iraq etc. This is a global problem where
Islamists increase to any significant number in a country.
Moderate followers of Muhammad in Britain want to live in
peace but the fundamentalists within their ranks will impose
Sharia law once they are in the majority. It has already been
implemented in some areas of Britain, even though Muslims
only make up about 6% of our population in 2012. On the
other hand, Jews have no problem with other religions in their
land, as seen by the 1.5 million Muslim Arabs living in the
State of Israel with freedom to practice their faith and having
full voting rights.

With the so called "Arab Spring" taking place in the
Middle East, the fundamentalists are rubbing their hands
with glee at the West supporting the removal of certain Arab
dictators in order to encourage democracy. Our leaders do
not understand that Islam is not interested in our western
style democracy where elected representatives make laws by
majority consent. Muslim leaders are not required to make
new laws but to impose Sharia law based on the Koran, which
is highly repressive and cruel as seen by over 1 million (20%)
Muslim Arabs. A Christian minister had a vision towards the
end of 2011 describing the current situation in the Middle
East. The Arab dictators were pictured as snakes but a larger
snake, i.e. Islam, devoured them all. From the frying pan into
the fire!

It should be stressed that it is not the Muslim people who
are the problem, but the teachings of Islam. There are many
good, upright men and women in the Muslim world, as there
are in the Jewish and other communities around the globe.
Christians are called to love, pray for and help all but not
to ignore the injustices that are happening in the world.

There is no excuse for wrong actions, whether taken by Jew or Gentile, but we should not expect the Jews to act near perfectly whilst others commit major wrongs and very little, if anything, is said about it. For instance, the British and US armies have proportionately killed far more civilians in Iraq and Afghanistan than the Israeli Army has killed whilst defending the Jewish nation against Muslim rockets and suicide bombers, etc. Although the deaths caused by both our Allied troops and the Israeli Defence Force are unintentional, Western journalists report the former as collateral damage but the latter as terrible and reprehensible war crimes. One of the problems for the IDF is that Muslim fighters hide in houses with their wives and children, so it is almost impossible to avoid civilian casualties. There are countless human tragedies on all sides but God is working for the salvation of all men and sees everything. He is the final judge, before whom all will have to stand and give an account for their actions.

Regarding sins among the Jews, since the State of Israel was declared in 1948, they have killed more of their own babies through abortion than Hitler did in his gas chambers. We in the West and elsewhere cannot throw stones on this or countless other issues either. Every nation under the sun is fundamentally flawed before God and needs Jesus as its only hope of salvation. There is no place for us to judge but we can observe and see the rights and wrongs of what has happened. Jesus said,

"Let he who is without sin cast the first stone",

(John 8:7)

God will deal righteously with all mankind and has declared,

"It is mine to avenge (judge)*; I will repay, says the Lord"*
(Deut. 32:35)

On the subject of God's righteousness, it is worth saying that when the Jews first entered the land as a nation after their deliverance from Egypt around 1500 BC, Joshua met the captain (Hebrew "sar" meaning **a** leader or captain but not **the** overall leader) of the Lord's army standing before him with a drawn sword (probably the Archangel Michael). Some say this was a manifestation of Jesus but I believe it was an angelic type of Jesus, just as the three angels that visited Abraham were a type of the Trinity, Gen.18:1-2. The main point I want to make is that the angel told Joshua he was not for them or against them but he was on the Lord's side, the side of absolute righteousness. And so it is today. God will not tolerate injustice by the Israeli government, Fatah, Hamas or anyone else in the whole world.

The only true and lasting answer for both Jew and Muslim is found in Christ, for it is uniquely through Him that God makes of the two *"one new man", Eph. 2:15.*

3 *The Three Major Covenants between God and the Jewish Nation*

God always keeps every promise He makes, but a covenant signed in blood, known as "cutting covenant", is a particularly special, all encompassing group of promises, specifically designed to bring the believer into a loving and secure relationship with Him. God made three of these covenants with the Jews. Every animal sacrifice commanded in the feasts of God was not only designed to keep the Jews righteous before Him but also to show the many aspects of the supreme sacrifice that Jesus was to make at Calvary, Heb. 9:22. Modern man has largely lost the understanding of blood sacrifice, but the born again believer becomes ever more aware and thankful for the enormity of suffering that Jesus endured in laying His life down and shedding His priceless life-giving blood for the world's sins.

God called Abram to Canaan, renamed him Abraham, and "cut covenant" with him, Gen. 15:8-12. This involved making several promises to the Patriarch, his son Isaac, his grandson

Jacob and his descendants. God purposed to bless the whole world through the Jews. Those that blessed them would be blessed and those who cursed them (Heb. *qala*) God would curse (Heb. *arar*), Gen. 12:2-3. These blessings and curses are still operative today upon those who are for or against both the Jews and the true Church – born again Gentiles become spiritual sons of Abraham through faith in Christ, Gal. 3:29. Those that curse either group are on a collision course with the Almighty, which will culminate in the events outlined in the book of Revelation.

As indicated, there are two different Hebrew words used by God in Genesis 12:3 but both are translated as "curse" in English. His response to those who would *"qala"* Israel and the born-again Church, meaning "to treat with low esteem or be abusive to", is to *"arar"* them, meaning "to strongly curse" (Young's Concordance). Even some Christians fall into this category when they unjustifiably speak ill of Israel and the body of Christ.

God promised to make the Jewish nation great and to give them a land flowing with milk and honey if they would only walk wholeheartedly with Him. His grace towards them was designed to be such a tremendous witness to all the surrounding nations that the Jews would be held in awe and Gentiles would want to seek Yahweh and convert to worshipping Him. Tragically, this only happened to any significant extent under King David and during the first part of his son Solomon's reign. The kings after him generally went spiritually downhill with a few exceptions.

It was not until Jesus came and received the fullness of the Holy Spirit at the Jordan River that God was able to instigate more of His plan to bless Israel and the nations. He poured out His grace on the Jews who believed Jesus and dealt with man's disobedience through His suffering and death on the cross. This opened the way for all Jesus' followers to receive the Holy Spirit as promised through the prophet Joel, Joel 2:28-32, bringing them into a far greater fulfilment of the covenant He made with Abraham, to be blessed and to bless all the peoples of the earth, Gen. 12:3. After this spectacular event on the day of Pentecost, the Messianic Jewish Church was able to reach and change the Gentile world through this new and living way, beginning with Cornelius and his household. God had opened Peter's eyes to see that Gentiles were also made clean through faith in Christ, Acts 10, which brought them into the Abrahamic covenant as well as the believing Jews:

"He (Jesus) *redeemed us* (from the curse of the law) *in order that the blessing given to Abraham might come to the Gentiles through Christ Jesus, so that by faith we might receive the promise of the Spirit.*

(Galatians 3:14)

Further dimensions of these promises to Abraham will be seen in the Millennium, the 1,000 year reign of Christ, when we receive our resurrection bodies, and they will be completely fulfilled when believers are placed on the new earth which has yet to be created.

God introduced the Mosaic Law at Mount Sinai through Moses, Ex. 24, to reveal not only to the Jews but to all mankind just how dreadfully sinful we are. It demonstrated the need for sacrifice in order for a person to be in right standing with Him and detailed the minimum standard of conduct required for Jews to walk with their God. This was highlighted by Isaiah who had a remarkably close relationship with God and received amazing insights into His plans. Despite this intimacy he said that, in the light of the law, his own righteousness was as filthy rags, Isaiah 64:6.

Later, God introduced the New Covenant through the shed blood of Jesus, Matt. 26:26-29. His death on the cross was the ultimate sacrifice, as it dealt once and for all with the sin problem and brought everlasting righteousness to all those who believe and follow Him, providing we continue in the faith. This Covenant enables both Jew and Gentile to reign in life through faith in Christ as part of God's plan to restore mankind to Himself.

It is very important to see that God made the New Covenant with the Jews and not the Gentiles. Jeremiah prophesied the following to the whole Jewish nation, not just to those who walked with God:

> *"The days are coming," declares the LORD, "when I will make a new covenant with the house of Israel and with the house of Judah."*
>
> (Jeremiah 31:31)

Thus, we cannot treat them as if they are no longer important to God since Christ came. Replacement Theology says the Jews have lost their special status before God through their rejection of Christ and are now just another nation needing salvation. It is true they need to receive the gospel to be saved, but the Bible makes it clear that the nation remains special before God because *"the gifts and the calling of God are irrevocable* (without repentance)", *Rom. 11:29.*

So, the Abrahamic, Mosaic and New Covenants were the three that God "cut" in blood with Israel. It is the Abrahamic covenant that inextricably links the Jews and born again Church together. Not only are Christians living in the first of these covenants as spiritual sons of Abraham, but the Mosaic one is also operative today, as I will show. There were several other promises made to the Jews in addition to these. For instance, God said David would always have one of his descendants on the throne, but this was not a promise made with blood.

Jews who truly believed the words of both the Abrahamic and Mosaic Covenants were walking with God before Jesus came and were the cultivated olive tree, *"the Israel of God", Gal. 6:16.* Not only were they called by God but they had responded to their calling by faith. On the other hand, unbelieving Jews since Abraham were broken off from this special tree because of their unbelief and it is on this point that both Replacement and Pro Israeli believers are confused. Many of the latter believe all Jews before Christ were saved regardless of faith and a few even believe they still are since Christ if they follow the law. God raised up many prophets during Old Testament times to preach the truth and restore Jews who had discarded their faith. As they repented and believed God's Word, they were grafted back in. Since Christ, Jews who reject the divinity and the work of Jesus on the cross are similarly cut off but are grafted back into the tree if they turn to their Messiah Jesus, Rom. 11:24.

Crucial to understanding Israel's history and her situation today is recognising that God's covenant to Abraham still includes the land. Just as the introduction of the Mosaic Covenant with its feasts and special days did not nullify any

promises made to Abraham, similarly there is nothing in the
New Covenant which detracts from them either. Herein lies
another major misunderstanding in Replacement Theology
and the root cause of this is the failure to understand the
role of the Mosaic Covenant since Jesus brought in the New
Covenant. Jesus said:

> *"I have not come to abolish the law but to fulfill it ...*
> *and **until heaven and earth disappear nothing will be***
> ***removed from the law until all is fulfilled** ... whoever*
> *breaks the commandments and teaches men to do so will*
> *be called least in the kingdom".*
>
> (Matthew 5:17-19)

Here, Jesus was teaching that the law would still stand until
heaven and earth disappear and all is fulfilled. His last words
on the cross were *"It is finished", John 19:30.* However,
this did not mean the law was finished with, but that His
sacrificial substitutional death had paid the price for the sins
of the whole world! Although Jesus did indeed fulfil the law,
there are many other things in end-time prophecy that God is
in the process of bringing about, as outlined in the books of
Revelation, Ezekiel, Daniel etc. *"All"* is not yet fulfilled.

The book of Hebrews confirms that the law has not been
abolished but that *"he* (Jesus) *has made the first* (Mosaic)
covenant obsolete", Heb. 8:13. The writer was discussing the
differences between the Old and New Covenants and so called
the Mosaic one the "first", even though it was actually the
second of the three major covenants God made with the Jews.
We know an obsolete car still works perfectly well although

it has been superseded by a superior model. One still has the choice of which car to drive!

Jesus fulfilled every aspect of the law and, as we walk by the Holy Spirit through faith in Christ, God considers that believers meet every requirement of the law as well.

> *"... that the righteous requirements of the law might be fully met in us,who do not live according to the sinful nature but according to the Spirit".*

(Romans 8:4)

Born again believers have not only been *"redeemed from the curse of the law", Gal. 3:13,* but also from the law of sin and death which was brought on the human race because of Adam's deliberate rebellion against God, Rom. 8:2. On being crucified with Christ, we are now free from this initial curse, Rom. 6:6. As we live by faith in what Jesus has done for us at the cross, we find we are dead to sin, although still subject to physical death until we receive our resurrection body.

> *"What shall we say, then? Shall we go on sinning so that grace may increase? By no means! We are those who have died to sin; how can we live in it any longer?*

(Romans 6:1-2)

Even more amazing is that born again believers stand before God, not just as if they had fulfilled the law, but in the perfection that Jesus lived in. This is a far higher standard as He led a totally sinless life, far above that which the law demanded, Heb.10:14. When we are born again, God makes a divine exchange and not only takes our sins but gives us His righteousness in Christ. We become new creatures in Christ, 2 Cor.5:17-21! It does not stop there, as God has also raised us up to sit and reign with Him in heavenly places!

"And God raised us up with Christ and seated us with him in the heavenly realms in Christ Jesus."

(Ephesians 2:6)

As far as His suffering was concerned, Jesus also went much further than the law required when He was sacrificed for us. The animals in the Old Testament were killed in a quick and painless way but Jesus was flogged with the Roman 39 lashes, wore a crown of thorns, carried His cross to Calvary and was nailed to it at 9 am on the morning of the Jewish Passover. He suffered excruciating pain for a further six hours before giving up his spirit at 3 pm, Mark 15:25-39. The law stipulated the punishments of hardship, pain, sickness, separation from God and finally death. Jesus suffered these that we might enjoy forgiveness, righteousness, healing and health in Him. Jesus suffered these that we might enjoy forgiveness, righteousness, healing and health in Him This breaking of His body and spilling of His blood wrought healing for us in spirit, soul and body. But we will not experience any of the benefits unless we live by the Spirit through faith in His Word.

Jesus not only fulfilled the Mosaic law and lived in perfection, but He introduced a new law!

"A new command I give you: Love one another. As I have loved you, so you must love one another."

(John 13:34)

The requirement of the law was only to love one another as we love ourselves. But now we are commanded to love each other as Christ loved the Church and laid His life down for her. This is not just for a husband towards his wife but for every member in the Church towards each other, whether single or not. He raised the bar on many other issues as well such as murder, adultery etc. In the New Covenant how we deal with thoughts is just as important as our actions.

His standard is, of course, totally impossible to practice in our old self but it is entirely possible through the gift of faith, the Holy Spirit and His great and precious promises. Through this abundant grace towards us, believers can *"participate in the divine nature and escape the corruption in the world caused by evil desires", 2 Pet. 1:4.*

So, to whom is the law speaking now that Jesus has fulfilled it? The answer is found in Paul's teaching to the Church in Rome. He saw that the law still applied to every Jew who rejected Jesus, even up to today. By refusing Him they are, by default, driving the obsolete vehicle and so remain under the law!

"all who sin under the law will be judged by the law."

(Romans 2:12)

This is the key revelation to unlock our understanding on the present position of Israel before God since Jesus introduced the New Covenant, and why the nation has suffered so much.

It means that since Jesus' time on earth, the Jews have continued to be judged by the law as a nation because the majority of them, including their high priest, rejected Him as their Messiah. Their continued rejection has had truly horrendous consequences as we have seen over the last two millennia. It even led to the Holocaust. *"I will scatter you among the nations and will draw out my sword and pursue you", Lev. 26:33!* But be sure, all the sins perpetrated against the Jews will be severely judged, even as they themselves have been justly judged. Unfortunately, Messianic Jews have had to suffer many hardships along with their rebellious Jewish brothers. This principle of the righteous suffering along with the unrighteous is seen through the Bible, for instance in Daniel's situation. Although he was totally obedient to God, he was exiled to Babylon along with all the rebellious Jews and suffered their disgrace.

Replacement Theology is correct in saying that God dispersed the Jews in 70 AD for rejecting Jesus. This was their punishment according to the Mosaic law, which decreed exile from the land for deliberate, stubborn and persistent disobedience. It was definitely not because He had cut them off as a special people. Also critical to understanding the situation is to see that God did not take the land from the Jews but He took the Jews from the land! Under the law, the land still belongs to them even during exile into other nations, as it was given them through the Abrahamic covenant, Lev. 26:42-45, Deut. 30:1-10 etc.

If one studies in detail how God calculates judgment periods, which we will look at in chapters 6, 7 and 8, it becomes clear that the Jews' second exile is ending in our day and that God is consequently drawing them back to the land. This is what the Lord showed me in Israel through the vision of the two long lines crossing each other – judgment coming off the nation of Israel and His restoration increasing.

Replacement Theology finds it difficult to reconcile how God can bring the Jews back to the land today, when most of them are still far from Him. Again, one has to understand that God is applying judgment according to the law which said that once the punishment period was over, He would remember the covenant made with their forefathers to bring them back, Leviticus 26:45 etc. Although the Jews have not yet repented on a national scale, God promised to do this even while their hearts are still hard towards Him, Ezekiel 36! He went on to say in this chapter that once they are in the land, He will bring them to repentance, taking away a heart of stone and giving them a new heart which, since the New Covenant, is only through faith in Christ, Ezek. 36:26. Praise God, many Jews have come to Jesus without having yet returned to Israel but we are going to see a work of God in the Jewish nation which will confound the world.

Israel's spiritual leaders have consistently missed the vital point that living under the law involves faith, Rom. 9:31-32. From this flows the ability to hear the Spirit explaining what the Word of God is saying. The law is the schoolmaster which points the individual to Christ, Gal. 3:24, and on into a relationship with God. On receiving Him, the Jew immediately moves into grace. Paul said that after his own conversion he was no longer under the law and so was completely free from having to fulfil it himself! For instance, the law required a man to go up to Jerusalem three times a year to observe the feasts, Deut. 16:16, but after his conversion, Paul only went there four times and never to celebrate the feasts or perform any of the law's requirements.

On one of these occasions, many years after his conversion, he was personally instructed by God to go up to Jerusalem, Acts 20:22 and Gal. 2:1. This was in spite of prophecies warning that he would be arrested and bound by the authorities, Acts 21:11. Paul was not only prepared to be imprisoned and beaten for the gospel's sake but to die for it. God saw this and made it part of His greater plan for Paul to witness to the rulers in the capital, the region and then in Rome, Acts 9:15 and 23:11. He wanted to arrive in Jerusalem, if possible, by Pentecost, Acts 20:16, as he knew many Jews would be there and he could give testimony to his conversion, Acts 21:39 to 23:11. By that time there were thousands of Messianic Jews in the city headed up by the apostle James and the other Church leaders, all still zealous for the law. The Orthodox Sanhedrin had come to tolerate the new Church to some extent because of this observance. Although the Church leaders embraced Paul as a true believer, his view that it was not necessary for Messianic Jews to keep the law was still controversial to them, Acts 21:20-21. They were frightened that the Jewish Council would clamp down on them and persecute the Church for associating with him. So they devised a ploy that Paul should join four Messianic Jews in the Temple who had made a vow. He would join in their purification rites and pay the authorities the required money so they could have their heads shaved, Acts 21:23-24. The Church leaders hoped this would make the authorities think Paul was keeping the law and its feasts. If he had already been doing so, this ruse would have been unnecessary. Paul complied with their idea, not wanting to cause any unnecessary trouble. He believed that in due course the Holy Spirit would show James and the rest of the Messianic Church the truth of what he was teaching about

Jesus having fulfilled the law. Indeed, James did eventually understand, and his letter written to Messianic Jews many years later never encouraged them to observe the Mosaic law but just to keep the spirit of it i.e. *"love your neighbor as yourself", James 2:8* etc.

It is on this subject of Jews keeping the feasts that many Pro-Israeli Christians stumble. Some evangelists and prophets lay particular emphasis on certain days as if God is still working to the Mosaic calendar and doing special things on these days. However, since that first Pentecost of the Church age when the Holy Spirit came on the Messianic believers, we are now to be led by Him into maturity rather than remain as a schoolchild, Gal. 4:1-7. This is the teaching thrust of the whole New Testament. It is good and important, however, to be aware of what Moses instructed and to understand the first five books of the Old Testament. There are many lessons within the law to show us God's thoughts on various issues. We limit our understanding by not reading it.

As discussed, the stark reality for zealous Jews who have rejected Jesus, both then and now, was taught by Jesus when He said *"If you believed Moses, you would believe me", John 5:46.* In other words, Jews who reject Jesus do not actually believe Moses in their hearts, even though many are deeply involved with observing Judaism.

When Paul wrote to the Ephesians saying *"He abolished in His flesh on the cross the law with its commandments", Eph. 2:15*, he was meaning that the law is abolished as far as every born again believer is concerned, whether Jew or Gentile, because Jesus fulfilled it for us – praise God! But it still applies to every Jew who rejects Jesus.

"For through the law, I died to the law so that I might live for God." Gal. 2:19. In Paul's sincerity of heart to God and the law, he was led to a revelation of Jesus and on trusting Him, the Holy Spirit crucified him with Christ.

Paul said,

I have been crucified with Christ and I no longer live, but Christ lives in me. The life I now live in the body, I live by faith in the Son of God, who loved me and gave himself for me. I do not set aside the grace of God, for if righteousness could be gained through the law, Christ died for nothing!"

(Galatians 2:19-21)

The same meaning is found in Colossians:

"He forgave us all our sins, having cancelled the written code, with its regulations, that was against us."

(Colossians 2:14)

It is only as we believe in Jesus that the cancellation comes into effect because we are then crucified with Christ and die to the law. Not only crucified, but buried and raised with Him in our spirit to live on His side of the cross in heaven! The same interpretation applies to *"Christ is the end of the law"*, *Rom. 10:4.* Again, the law has not ended for the unbelieving Jew, only for the Messianic Jew.

God earnestly desired that the whole Jewish nation receive Christ 2,000 years ago so they could have enjoyed the benefits of the New Covenant as a people, rather than the misery and death so many of them have unnecessarily suffered. The unbelief by the majority of their leaders and people caused Jesus untold grief and pain when He looked at the crowds on His last visit to the temple. He was speaking to them as a nation not as individuals:

> *"O Jerusalem, Jerusalem, you who kill the prophets and stone those sent to you, how often I have longed to gather your children together, as a hen gathers her chicks under her wings, but you were not willing. Look, your house is left to you desolate.* **For I tell you, you will not see me again until you say, "Blessed is He** (Jesus) **who comes in the name of the Lord."**
>
> (Matthew 23:37-39)

I have highlighted Jesus' very significant words in the above quotation that the Jews will not see Him again until they believe He is their Lord. We know from other scriptures that the hope of His second advent is assured, and so Jesus was effectively saying that their national conversion will definitely happen before He is seen coming in the clouds with great glory! This is confirmed by Zechariah as he described the end-time events surrounding Jerusalem, when the Jews have come to Christ and are on fire for Him before His return:

> *On that day I will make the clans of Judah like a fire pot in a woodpile, like a flaming torch among sheaves. They will consume right and left all the surrounding peoples, but Jerusalem will remain intact in her place.*
>
> (Zechariah 12:6)

On Jesus' triumphant entry into Jerusalem during the last week of His ministry, many did believe in Him but most did not. Even among those who welcomed Him, a large number only saw Him as a prophet coming in the name of the Lord, Matt. 21:11. If the whole nation had believed in Him 2,000 years ago, we would have seen an entirely different scenario played out in the Church age with the Romans being unable to destroy Jerusalem in 70 AD, and Israel living in the riches of Christ. This would have made the Gentile nations extremely jealous, causing the world to turn to God in greater measure than we have seen thus far, rather than Gentiles believers now being required to make the Jews jealous in order to bring them to Christ! When Paul wrote regarding the remnant of Israel, *"and so all Israel will be saved"*, Rom. *11:26,* he was referring to those Jews who survive the End-time Tribulation and come to Christ on a national scale, as further prophesied by Zechariah, chapter 12:7-14. This mass conversion must happen before Jesus returns and will result in multitudes more Gentiles being drawn into the kingdom, as the Jews join us en masse in preaching the gospel!

The world is entering a time of labour pains before this glorious return. These contractions will become more and more severe and frequent but within them God will bring forth the finishing touches to a triumphant and radiant Church on earth, a bride fit for her Saviour and King! This will include the whole surviving remnant of Jews, including the 144,000 who are on fire for Jesus in a special way, Rev. 7:4 and 14:1, and who, like the apostle Paul, have accepted God's will of celibacy rather than marriage. Through all the traumas, God reveals whether a man has built his house on sand or on the Rock, which is Jesus Christ. We are going to see God shake the world so that everything which is not of Him will collapse (even the value of gold according to a prophecy by the late David Wilkerson) to reveal what is unshakable i.e. those rooted and grounded in His Kingdom through faith in Christ.

> *"The foundations of the earth shake, the earth is broken*
> *up and the earth is split asunder."*
>
> (Isaiah 24:18-19)

In Christ we find *"there is neither Jew nor Greek* (Gentile)*"*, *Gal. 3:28*, although very importantly there is still a distinction between them in the natural realm. Similarly, just as there is neither male nor female spiritually in Christ, an obvious natural difference remains, as you may have noticed! However, Gentile believers do become spiritual sons of Abraham as far as relationship with God is concerned and are *"no longer strangers to the covenants"*, *Ephes. 2:12*. Furthermore, in Christ our Father has *"blessed us in the heavenly realms with every spiritual blessing"*, *Ephes. 1:3*, and even more amazingly we are *"fellow heirs with Christ"*, *Rom. 8:17*.

There has been a recent concentration in certain parts of the Church about "returning Christians to their Jewish roots". The Holy Spirit has always taught on this, but there have been misunderstandings by some as to what these roots are referring to. They are Abraham, who is the father of faith, Rom. 4:17, Isaac and Jacob. Abraham believed God and was even prepared to sacrifice his greatest treasure on earth, Isaac. Are we willing to sacrifice our greatest treasure? The book of Romans is a masterpiece covering the main aspects of the Christian faith for all of us to discover our roots. God does not want us to go back to observing the law with its feasts as the New Testament writers explained at length. Moses is part of the trunk of the cultivated olive tree but not the roots!

Let us not forget that God had to instigate the Reformation to extricate the Church from Old Covenant Christianity. He is still working to bring the true Church to maturity in Christ through an ever greater understanding of New Testament teaching, that we might walk in the Light even as He is in the Light.

4 *Modern Jewish History*

In this chapter I am seeking to redress the bias against the Jewish nation which has dogged them for centuries and still continues today. Hopefully this will show us something of their side of the story.

The original objective of the Balfour Declaration in 1917 was for the whole of Palestine to be a homeland for the Jewish people without prejudicing the civil and religious rights of existing non-Jewish communities. In 1922, the League of Nations, forerunner to the United Nations, gave Great Britain the Mandate to implement the Declaration. It was agreed with the nations that Israel would be a single state covering the whole area with equal rights for both Jew and Arab.

At the end of WWI in 1918, there were about five hundred thousand Arabs and seventy thousand Jews living in the land. This ratio was not reflected in Jerusalem, as there were more Jews living in the city than Arabs. The intention within the Mandate was that immigration levels of Jews would be dependent on the economic capability of the country to cope with the number entering the land. It was clearly understood that this would lead to a Jewish majority in the land, but this was not considered a problem by the League of Nations including the Muslim Arab leaders who had fought with the Allied Armies to liberate Palestine from the Turkish Empire. Great optimism followed the Mandate due to the expectation that Jews would significantly increase the material prosperity of everyone living in the country, especially benefitting the largely poor Arab population. The true moderate Muslims welcomed the Jews back to their homeland and acknowledged their historic right to live there as a people. However, the fundamentalist Muslims started to fight against both the indigenous Jews and those returning to the land. It was they who later colluded with Hitler to devise ways of exterminating the Jews.

The Peel Commission, set up in 1936 to investigate the grievances which had arisen on both sides after implementation of the Mandate, concluded that because of the armed reaction by militant Muslims to the Jews, only a two-state solution might work. This was contrary to the Mandate which stated "a national homeland for the Jews" in a single state comprising both Jews and Arabs. Several other factors such as the threat to oil supplies, the possible loss of the Suez Canal and war looming, led the British, in 1939, to impose an immigration limit of 75,000 Jews per annum for five years and then no more. Most Western Governments also refused Jews entry into their countries and consequently they were trapped in Germany, Poland etc. Many thousands who tried to escape to Israel to avoid the vicious Nazi persecution were forcefully turned back. This resulted in hundreds of thousands more Jews being transported like cattle in goods wagons to Hitler's infamous gas chambers. The Vichy government in France also instructed their police to round up Jews and send them to the death camps in Germany and Poland. All this was a direct result of Britain breaking her internationally agreed legal duty and promise that Jews should be free to live in Israel. At the height of the slaughter, somewhere around 20,000 a day were murdered in Hitler's death camps. If one includes all Jews executed elsewhere in Europe by the Nazis, Stalin etc., the overall number exterminated is significantly greater than 6 million.

In the thirties, Arabs had poured into Israel from the surrounding countries, particularly Jordan. This unexpected influx of Arabs had not been envisaged in the Mandate. Also, the spiritual awareness that had been present through Bible believing Christians in the British Government in 1917 had dramatically reduced by World War II. Consequently, there was much less spiritual understanding in the government during the 1939-1945 war regarding Satan's attempts to counter God's restoration of Israel. The British, in their self interest, eventually threw up their hands in exasperation and handed the problem to the U.N. who voted in 1947 to divide the land into two states with Jerusalem as an international city. The British Government abstained from the vote, adding to the shame of reneging on earlier promises made to the Jews.

The concept of an Arab State for the Palestinians was an entirely new one, as there had never been an Arab community with its own government and country called Palestine. As explained earlier, it was thanks to Hadrian in 135 AD that the land was renamed Palestine rather than Israel as it had been known in both Old and New Testament times. Since then, both Jews and Arabs living in the area were referred to as Palestinians. Due to the disinterest of its Ottoman rulers after Suleiman the Magnificent died in 1566, Jerusalem and the rest of the area became a neglected and impoverished part of southern Syria right up to the liberation of the city in 1917 by General Allenby in WW1.

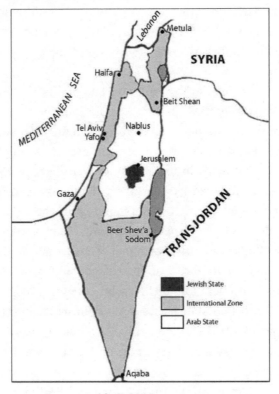

1947 U.N. vote

In 1947, the Jews accepted the UN two state solution but the Arabs rejected it. On the 14th of May 1948, the day after the last British troops had left, David Ben-Gurion, the socialist Prime Minister, declared the Jewish State. The following day, surrounding Muslim nations went to war against her. They intended to exterminate every Jew and take the whole land for the Arabs. The Muslim leaders instructed the Palestinians living in the land to evacuate their houses and leave the country whilst the Jews were annihilated. The plan was for the Palestinians to return later and take their pick of Jewish property anywhere in the land. The vast majority left but, as we know, the Jews, far from being annihilated, gained further areas and a wedge of land up to the western part of new Jerusalem which had not been granted to them by the U.N. The Jordanians invaded the West Bank and took control of Old Jerusalem on the eastern side. All the land surrounding the city had originally been allocated to the Palestinians, leaving several miles between the Jews and their beloved city.

This attack on Israel was an illegal act of war under international law and the perpetrators should have been prosecuted. Had they been tried, they would have been found guilty of invading a sovereign country as the Germans were after World War II. The Arab leaders from the belligerent nations could then have been punished and their military put under supervision until they could be trusted to work for peace. Instead, the world turned a blind eye to this injustice whereby the nations in question were allowed to increase their military capabilities and have since made further attempts to exterminate the Jews. The latest major threat comes from Iran which has declared its intention of wiping Israel off the map. They are busily enriching uranium and developing their missiles to carry nuclear warheads over Israel to achieve this evil desire.

The Palestinians have demanded compensation for the houses they chose to abandon, but it is really the responsibility of the neighbouring Arab nations to assimilate the refugees into their own countries, as they started the war against Israel in 1948 and caused the displacement problem by instructing the Palestinians to leave. Interestingly, the value of property lost by Jews who were forced to flee for their lives from the Muslim nations during the war is not far off that lost by the Palestinians. The tragedy is that if it were not for extremists stirring up the moderate Muslims to wage war against the Jews, both Jew and Arab would be living together in an extremely high level of prosperity in one country.

In the 1948 War of Independence, the Jordanians invaded Judea and Samaria, now referred to as the West Bank, and occupied it until they were driven back in 1967. They did little more for the Palestinians than renovate the Dome of the Rock and gild its top. However, they did come against the Jews, ethnically cleansing the area by killing those who did not immediately flee. During the occupation, 55 Jewish synagogues were destroyed leaving little freedom for faiths other than Islam. In the 1967 war, which was again started by the Arabs, the Jews liberated East Jerusalem and the West Bank from the Jordanians. All religions were once again free to practise their faith there under Israeli rule. Today, Palestinians largely govern themselves in the West Bank, and the Jewish settlements only cover 1.5% of the area. The only reason the I.D.F has put restrictions on freedom of movement through the checkpoints and the fence itself, is to try and stop terrorists murdering Jews. If the Arabs took responsibility for this, normal relations could be resumed and the barrier taken down.

I believe the reason things have gone so very wrong in the Middle East is mainly due to the teaching of Islam. God promised to bring the Jews back to Israel in the last days, so Satan has deceived the Muslims into believing that because the Jews rejected Jesus and the other prophets, they have somehow forfeited the land permanently and it now belongs to the sons of Ishmael. Satan knows from Ezekiel 36 and many other prophecies that Jesus will not return until the land is fully restored to the Jews, so he is mounting an all out attack to stop this from happening. The Bible also warns that the Jews have many great trials ahead of them, but just when it looks like the final curtain is coming down on them, Jesus will step in to destroy all the nations attacking Israel and throw Satan, the Great Deceiver, into prison. The book of Revelation tells us that an angel will *"seize the dragon, that ancient serpent, who is the devil, or Satan, and bind him for a thousand years. He threw him into the Abyss"*, Rev. 20:1-3.

Satan understands these scriptures only too well and wants to keep as many Christians as possible in the dark regarding Israel, the Jews and their return because he knows our prayers are effective against his evil schemes to thwart God's purposes. Replacement Theology plays into Satan's hands as it sees no requirement for the Jews to return to Israel. Although people are far more important to God than territory, He did promise the land to them. He will surely keep His promise whilst bringing as many as possible to saving faith in the process.

5 God's Decree over the Jews and Jerusalem

Looking back towards the end of the exile in Babylon, we find Daniel pouring out his heart in prayer to God for his people and their beloved city which he had not seen since his youth. He had been deported in the first year along with the royalty, nobles and craftsmen. Daniel had just read Jeremiah's prophecy that they would be held as prisoners in Babylon for 70 years and he realized that this judgment was nearly completed. God answered his earnest intercession by sending the angel Gabriel to make the extremely important decree over the Jews and Jerusalem, Dan. 9:24-27, quoted below.

Verse 24 gives an overall time scale for the prophecy, namely *"seventy sevens"*, which, when multiplied, makes 490 units of time. None of the events mentioned in the prophecy occurred within 490 days, weeks or months, but if this refers to years, then they start to fit into history.

[24] "Seventy 'sevens' (490 years) are decreed for your people and your holy city to finish transgression, to put an end to sin, to atone for wickedness, to bring in everlasting

*righteousness, to seal up vision and prophecy and to
anoint the Most Holy.*

*²⁵Know and understand this: From the time the
word goes out to restore and rebuild Jerusalem until
the Anointed One, the ruler, comes, there will be seven
'sevens'* (49 years), *and sixty-two 'sevens'* (434 years – a
total of 483 years). *It will be rebuilt with streets and a
trench, but in times of trouble* (rebuilding of the Temple
commenced on the Jews' return to Jerusalem in 535 BC
at the decree by Cyrus, Ezra 1:1. It was not until 444 BC
when the decree was made by Artaxerxes, another Persian
king, Neh. 2:1, that rebuilding the city started).

²⁶After the sixty-two 'sevens' (at the end of 483 years),
the Anointed One (Jesus) *will be put to death and will
have nothing* (483 years ended at His crucifixion without
Him being accepted as King by the Jews). *The people
of the ruler who will come will destroy the city and the
sanctuary. The end will come like a flood* (the Romans
under Caesar. His general, Titus, destroyed Jerusalem in
70 AD)*: War will continue until the end* (since then many
wars have been fought over Jerusalem, continuing after
our day, and will eventually culminate with the return of
Jesus), *and desolations have been decreed* (the Antichrist
will set himself up in the rebuilt temple and desecrate it).

²⁷He (the Antichrist) *will confirm a covenant with
(*or for) *many for one 'seven'* (the last 7 years). *In the
middle of the 'seven'* (3.5 years into it) *he will put an
end to* (Judaic) *sacrifice and offering. And at the temple
he will set up an abomination that causes desolation*
(the False Prophet will set up an image of the Antichrist,
Rev. 13:14-15), *until the end that is decreed is poured out*

on him (this last decree seals the Antichrist's fate of being cast into the lake of fire, Rev. 19:19-20). *"*

(Daniel 9:24-27)

Verse 26 says that after 483 years (49 + 434 = 483) *"the Anointed One will be put to death"*, which obviously refers to Jesus' horrendous crucifixion at Golgotha. It then predicts that Jerusalem would be destroyed along with the temple, referring to the city's siege and final destruction by Titus in 70 AD. But Titus never confirmed any covenant with or for the Jews and indeed, we have yet to see anything that fits the events of verse 27 when the Antichrist will *"confirm covenant"*. The original Hebrew in this verse does not state the definite or indefinite article i.e. whether it should read *"confirm **the** covenant"* or *"confirm **a** covenant"*, so the context must decide which article should be used. The NIV chooses to put "a" whereas the King James Bible has "the". When Daniel gives more information about the same end-time situation, he again refers to the abolition of sacrifice, Dan.12:11-12, so it seems more likely that *"confirm **the** covenant"* is meant. This would entail the reinstatement of temple sacrifice, not just a political agreement as is currently being sought between the Israelis and Palestinians. At the time of writing (2012) there is neither temple nor sacrifice but Scripture says we shall see both restored at some point. It will not be at God's instigation, however, as He has no need of a stone temple because the law has been fulfilled and Old Testament Levitical priests are no longer required (Heb. 7:11-28).

There is, therefore, a 2,000 year time gap between verses 26 and 27 of Daniel 9. Replacement Theology does not see this and says that all the events of verse 27 either happened in

70 AD or have been cancelled as God has written the Jews off for rejecting their Messiah, Jesus. Josephus, a Jewish historian living at the time who negotiated with the Romans, records the whole siege and destruction of Jerusalem in detail. He makes no mention of the Romans making or confirming a covenant with the Jews for seven years and then abolishing it three and a half years later. Titus did offer the Jews a truce in 70 AD but when the majority refused to surrender, he destroyed both city and temple, slaughtering men, women and children in that same year, not three and a half years later. Over 1 million Jews were killed in the campaign. Importantly, Josephus was a Jewish priest, so if these events had been a fulfilment of verse 27, especially in regard to the abomination in the temple, it would have been truly noteworthy and he would have recorded it.

There are some who believe that the abolition of sacrifice in verse 27 refers to the death of Jesus when the curtain was torn from top to bottom and God made the Levitical sacrifice obsolete. This school of thinking therefore believes that the first three and a half years of the last seven started with Jesus' baptism in the River Jordan and ended at the cross. This would mean Jesus *"confirmed covenant"* through this period. Firstly, He did not start confirming the Old Covenant then, as He observed the law during His whole life. He did indeed start implementing the covenant promises made to Abraham in His first year of ministry through the power of the Holy Spirit in teachings, healings, miracles etc. and He fulfilled the law throughout His 33 years on earth. But, also, the prophecy states that the crucifixion was at the end of 483 years, i.e. at the beginning of the last seven years and not half way through them. Therefore, this idea is not tenable. However, they do correctly believe the last three and a half years are yet to happen when the Antichrist reigns, as described from Revelation chapter six onwards.

The very reason God separated the last seven years from the first 483 years of the prophecy is because of the large time gap between the cross and these end years. We are left with no other possibility than that the final seven year period, often referred to as Daniel's 70th Week, is yet to run.

We know that God has already factored Satan's evil schemes into His perfect and righteous plans. But let me show you in more detail how God is working out His purposes through both the nation of Israel and the nations of this world to bring His Kingdom on earth as it is in heaven.

6 The Times of the Gentiles

Understanding the rather unusual phrase "times of the Gentiles" used by Jesus, Luke 21:24, will bring further clarification and meaning as to how God is dealing with the nation of Israel in our day. I will spend some time unpacking this scripture as it clearly confirms that because the Jews rejected Christ as a nation, God is still dealing with them according to the law given through Moses. We will then have a greater insight into how God has been, and still is, working through history.

During His last week in Jerusalem, Jesus made the dire prediction that the Jews would yet again face the judgment sword and be dispersed amongst the Gentile nations. This was due to the refusal by the High Priest, most of the elders and the majority of the nation to accept Jesus as their Messiah and King. He warned His disciples of the results of this stubbornness of heart saying:

> *"They* (the Jews) *will fall by the sword and will be taken as prisoners to all nations. Jerusalem will be trampled by the Gentiles until the times of the Gentiles are fulfilled".*
>
> (Luke 21:24)

But Jesus was also saying here that there **would** be an end to these humiliating years in exile.

It must be clearly understood that "the times of the Gentiles" do not refer to years when Gentiles come to Christ, but to the periods when God removed Israel's kings and brought Gentile powers to rule over the nation because of their extremely ungodly behaviour. This punishment had been spelt out to them in Leviticus 26 where Moses detailed the curses God would bring for stubborn and sustained rebellion to His Word. God promised to bless the Jews with abundance and increase their numbers if they obeyed Him wholeheartedly, but if they turned away in persistent disobedience, He would punish them severely:

> *"But if you will not listen to me and carry out all these commands, and if you reject my decrees and abhor my laws and fail to carry out all my commands and so violate my covenant, then I will do this to you: I will bring on you sudden terror, wasting diseases and fever that will destroy your sight and sap your strength. You will plant seed in vain, because your enemies will eat it. I will set my face against you so that you will be defeated by your enemies; those who hate you will rule over you, and you will flee even when no one is pursuing you."*
>
> (Leviticus 26:14-17)

The punishments were first applied when the Jews wandered for 40 years in the wilderness, and then several times after entering the Promised Land during the period of their judges when they forsook the Lord for foreign gods. During these times, God brought other nations to invade and steal their crops, as the Midianites did for seven years, Judges 6:1. Each time the Jews cried out to the Lord, He faithfully saved them. But after the kingdom had been divided because of Solomon's gross unfaithfulness to God, their kings and priests rebelled in a far more serious manner. The northern kingdom was exiled first and was sent to Assyria without a timescale for their return, but just over 100 years later the two southern tribes of Judah and Benjamin were expelled from the land into Babylon for a specific 70 year period. Jeremiah informs us that it was God who raised up the ruthless Babylonians to judge not only the Jews but also the surrounding nations as well.

> "Therefore the LORD Almighty says this: "Because you (Jews) have not listened to my words, I will summon all the peoples of the north and my servant Nebuchadnezzar king of Babylon," declares the LORD, "and I will bring them against this land and its inhabitants and against all the surrounding nations. I will completely destroy them and make them an object of horror and scorn, and an everlasting ruin."
>
> (Jeremiah 25:8-9)

King Jehoiakim suffered the humiliation of being the last Jewish monarch to exercise God-given authority in Jerusalem. He was unceremoniously stripped of his power by Nebuchadnezzar, the Babylonian king, who left him in charge as a puppet ruler. Most of the nobles, including Jehoiakin the deposed king's son, the prophet Daniel, as well as many craftsmen were forcibly taken away to Babylon that year. Unfortunately, Jehoiakim continued to do great evil even while God was punishing them. Nebuchadnezzar was infuriated by the king's behaviour and replaced him with his son Jehoiakin, who was brought back from Babylon to govern. Tragically, he continued in his father's sinful ways and the Lord declared him childless saying, *"Record this man childless... None of his offspring will sit on the throne of David"*, *Jer. 22:30*. He was duly replaced by his uncle, Zedekiah, who alas disobeyed God's Word as well. The disgrace of not having a king has been part of the Jews' just punishment ever since but, praise God, it will all change in the not too distant future.

During this initial 70 years judgment, the Lord continued to command the Jews, through Jeremiah, to repent from their gross sins of worshipping foreign gods. He had directed them to fully comply with the Babylonians in order to minimise loss of life. But still they took no notice, which forced God to impose the far heavier second step of judgment as detailed by Moses in Leviticus 26:18-46. I quote the first three verses below to show the massive seven fold or "seven times" increase in severity, designed to break down their stubborn pride. It is from this verse that Jesus took the word "times" when he described the punishment period "the times of the Gentiles".

> *"If after all this you will not listen to me, I will punish you for your sins seven times over. I will break down your stubborn pride and make the sky above you like iron and the ground beneath you like bronze.*
> *Your strength will be spent in vain, because your soil will not yield its crops, nor will the trees of your land yield their fruit."*

(Leviticus 26:18-20)

This "seven times over" punishment resulted in the torching and comprehensive destruction of Jerusalem and its temple, with the deaths of many thousands more Jews. The survivors were removed from the city and exiled to Babylon. Archaeologists and historians put this destruction firmly in the year 586 BC, 19 years after the capture of the city by the Babylonians in 605 BC, as the quote below states. All the devastating events against the once righteous and glorious city established by King David are recorded by Jeremiah in his book from chapter 25 onwards. They are also written in the book of Kings:

> *"On the seventh day of the fifth month, in the nineteenth year of Nebuchadnezzar king of Babylon, Nebuzaradan commander of the imperial guard, an official of the king of Babylon, came to Jerusalem. He set fire to the temple of the LORD, the royal palace and all the houses of Jerusalem. Every important building he burned down. The whole Babylonian army under the commander of the imperial guard broke down the walls around Jerusalem. Nebuzaradan the commander of the guard carried into exile the people who remained in the city, along with the rest of the populace and those who had deserted to the king of Babylon. But the commander left behind some of the poorest people of the land to work the vineyards and fields."*
>
> (2 Kings 25:8-12)

The humiliating 70 year exile, the first judgment, ended in 535 BC as God had promised, and the Jews returned to Jerusalem. However, as we will see, the second stage of judgment, as quoted above in Leviticus 26:18, was still in force even though they had come back and rebuilt the Temple and city. This further punishment for continuing to rebel whilst under the Babylonians is seen by the royal line of kings not being re-instated, foreign powers continuing to rule over them and the Holy Spirit not re-entering the rebuilt temple.

The second judgment, starting with the destruction of Jerusalem, is known as the Great Seven Times Punishment by those who study the chronology of Scripture, and is named after the "seven times" description in Lev. 26:18. On investigation, it is found to have a time element within it as well as an increase in severity, as seen by reading the remainder of the chapter. The phrase "seven times" or seven fold is repeated on four occasions within the chapter, Lev. 26:18, 21, 24 and 28. On looking at Israel's history, this repeat does not mean four different lots of punishment periods but that God varied His judgments within the single "seven times" period in accordance with the level of their sin.

To summarise: 605 BC was the start of 70 years of punishment when the Jews first lost their sovereignty. Then in 586 BC, the "seven times" punishment began with their removal from Jerusalem. Finally in 535 BC, although they returned to Jerusalem to rebuild the walls and the temple etc, foreign powers continued to rule over them. The reason for giving all these details is to show that just as the punishment periods were imposed in stages, so God is concluding them by specific steps of restoration in our day.

Jewish history reveals that since 605 BC Gentile rule over the Jews has been continuous. The Babylonians were conquered by King Cyrus the Great of Persia in 535 BC. It was he who proclaimed the God-inspired decree for the Jews to return to Jerusalem and rebuild the temple, Ezra 1. Many Jews from the two southern tribes did return, as recorded by Ezra and Nehemiah, but a large number remained in several territories of the Persian Empire, as described in the book of Esther. The Persians were followed by the Greeks, whose empire was eventually divided between Alexander the Great's four generals after his untimely death. Two of them died. One became king of the territory to the north of Israel (the Seleucid Syrian Empire) and the other to the south (the Ptolemy Egyptian Dynasty). Israel was initially under the northern king but the descendants of these two frequently fought one another for dominance so the relatively powerless Jews switched masters according to the fortunes of each dynasty.

Antiochus IV, a later descendant of the northern Greek Seleucids and a particularly evil king, brutally attacked the Jews, seeking to destroy Judaism. As we know, Satan has a unique hatred towards the Jews and motivated Antiochus to defile their temple with pig sacrifices offered to his god Zeus. In 167 BC, Mattathias, a Jewish priest, together with all his sons, headed up a successful revolt against this abomination. They became known as the Maccabees, meaning hammer, due to their strong resistance to Antiochus. In 164 BC, after three vicious years of fighting, they gained back control of Jerusalem and the temple was duly cleansed. Amazingly, the Greek desecration by Antiochus had been prophesied by Daniel nearly 400 years earlier whilst he was exiled in Babylon, Dan. 11:21-35. Verses 33-35 of the chapter refer to the godly Jews at that time who refused to renounce their faith even under extreme torture. They heroically resisted even to their cruel and violent deaths.

As a matter of interest, it was during the rededication of the temple in 164 BC, following the Antiochus IV defilement, that tradition says the seven-stemmed Menorah miraculously burned for eight days in the temple. There had only been enough ceremonial oil prepared for one day but it lasted for the whole eight day period until a fresh supply was available. This notable event is recorded in the Talmud and is still celebrated today by Jews at Chanukah (pronounced Hanukah, meaning dedication) on the 25th of Kislev, the ninth month. It's called the Festival of Lights in their calendar.

During a brief period of relative freedom whilst the Greeks and Egyptians fought each other, the Maccabees introduced a monarchy. But these kings were not from David's royal genetic line as the Jews were still under the judgment of being denied a God ordained legitimate king of their own. One day soon, when the punishments fully come to an end, God will graciously restore a king to them, Jer. 33:17-26. His name is Jesus – King of Kings and Lord of Lords!

Later, when Antiochus V succeeded his father, he offered the Jews a truce rather than retribution, but he did tear down the walls of Jerusalem just in case they caused him trouble. He wanted to demonstrate who was in charge, even though he had left them to their own devices. So the Jews remained under either Seleucid or Ptolemaic rule during the whole post-Alexander era until 63 BC when the ruthless Roman armies conquered the Greeks and took Jerusalem into their empire. The Romans saw it was to their advantage to let the Jews keep their "kings" as puppet rulers, among whom were the infamous Herods of Jesus' time on earth. Therefore, all these years are part of the continuous punishment under Gentile domination.

The Roman Empire purposely divided into two in 395 AD for ease of government with the eastern Byzantine part continuing to rule over Israel. The Persian Sassanids attacked the eastern half, substantially weakening their hold over the city and in 614 AD they massacred some 80,000 Byzantine Christians in Jerusalem. Although the latter fought back and held the city, they were a spent force which made it relatively easy for the Muslims to take Jerusalem in 638 AD.

Meanwhile Muhammad had started to preach his new religion in 610 AD. After he died through poisoning in 632 AD, the Muslim armies took much of the Middle East and Jerusalem in 638 AD. The Jews remained under Muslim rule and were forced to pay the Zakat tax levied on all unbelievers under Islamic rule. In 1099, the spiritualy unenlightened Roman Catholic Crusaders captured the city by force, slaughtering Muslim and Jew alike. The wars were initiated because the Muslims had denied Catholic pilgrims access to their church, the Holy Sepulchre, in Jerusalem and the Jews were slaughtered for rejecting and condemning Jesus to death. The Catholics held Jerusalem for over 100 years and have much to answer for regarding the terrible image of Christianity portrayed to both Muslims and Jews. Various Muslim groups then seized back the city, with the Turks taking control in 1517. Finally, our Allied troops entered Jerusalem in 1917 during the First World War. In 1922 the League of Nations gave Great Britain the Mandate to govern the whole land, and following the 1947 vote by the United Nations, the newly born State of Israel finally came into being on May 14th 1948.

This very long and tortuous period of shame under foreign rule is part of *"the times of the Gentiles"* that Jesus spoke of in Luke chapter 21. In my book Almost Midnight, I have included more detail about how God decided upon the length of each judgment against the Jews. However, I will give an overview of the salient points in the next chapter to further prove that God is still dealing with the Jews according to His law through Moses.

7 *Steps of Judgment and Restoration*

The first point to understand in deducing their length is that when the Bible says "years" without any qualification, it always means normal solar ones of 365.25 days. For example the 70 years of Babylonian rule were solar years as there is no indication to the contrary.

On closer study of the scriptures, we discover that when God imposed the second and more severe judgment, the "seven times" punishment of Levitcus 26:18, He started to use the 30 day Gentile calendar month to calculate its duration. This was further emphasising that the Jews were to be in total subjection to foreign Gentile rule.

In the ancient world, each year started with the first new moon after the spring equinox, when the lengths of day and night are equal. Every month also started at a new moon but was considered as lasting 30 days rather than the actual 29.5 days of a lunar cycle, because it was too awkward for them to calculate the half days. Twelve months therefore totalled 360 days, and were thought of as a circle to show the repeating cycle of the seasons in each year. From this the

Babylonians developed the concept of 360 degrees in a circle – a degree for every day of the year. Also in their calculations, they used 60 as a base number being $1/6^{th}$ of 360 and easily divisible by a number of factors, 30, 20, 15 etc. It is from this base that we have 60 seconds in a minute and 60 minutes in an hour.

It was not until the Exodus from Egypt, when God introduced the law with its feasts, that the Jews dropped the 360 day year. The law given through Moses did not concern itself with how many days there were in a month or a year, but continued to start each month with a new moon. The first day of the month would also be the start of a new week (our Sunday) thus ensuring the Passover and Tabernacles always started on the evening of the 14th day (our Friday) in the first and seventh months. Moses was instructed to begin their calendar from the first new moon when the barley was green and nearly ready for harvest, Ex. 12:2 and 13:4. This initial month was called Abib, meaning green ears. Later during their exile, the Jews adopted the Babylonian name, Nisan, along with much of their captors' Aramaic language. The Passover lamb was sacrificed at sunset on the 14th of the first month (our Friday evening) and this commenced a Passover Sabbath (the Jewish day always commenced at sunset). To distinguish it from a normal one it was called a High Sabbath, and it ended on the Saturday evening at sunset on the 15th day. Barley was the earliest crop to ripen and God's law required the first sheaf from it to be cut on the 16th day (our Sunday). This day marked the beginning of the Feast of First Fruits. A sheaf was cut from the green barley and waved before the Lord with much praise and thanksgiving for the harvest of their first spring crop, Lev. 23:10-14. The rest of the barley could then be gathered in. First Fruits lasted seven weeks and one day, i.e. fifty days. On the last day they celebrated Pentecost and gave thanks for the harvest of wheat, the second main crop of the year. Linking the beginning of First Fruits to the barley harvest always kept their feasts in sync with the weather. If it was a particularly cold winter and the barley was very late, they just skipped a month to the next new moon and that became their first month. So the Jewish calendar was 354 days (12 x 29.5) and the Gentile calendar was considered 360 days (12 x 30). The other days of the 365.25 day solar year were just ignored in both schemes.

The very unusual phrase "time, times and half a time" occurs on several occasions in both the Old and New Testaments and we will look at it in more detail in the next chapter. Suffice to say at this stage, the word "time" describes a 360 day year and God started to use them in His calculations when the "seven times" punishment of Leviticus 26:18-20 began in 586 BC with the destruction of Jerusalem. Seven of these judgment years makes 2,520 days. However, foreign rule over the Jews lasted for a great many more years than this and was over a continuous period. So we need to take into account another principle God employs, when appropriate, in deciding the length of punishment to fit the level of disobedience. This is the year for a day principle. For instance, the Israelites spent 40 years in the wilderness for not believing they could overcome the giants and strongholds with God's help. They did not believe Joshua's good report – they did not mix God's Word with faith, Heb. 4:1-3. Accordingly, they were kept in the wilderness one year for each day the spies were in the land, Num. 14:34. Throughout the Bible we learn that remaining in unbelief is sin, as Paul clearly pointed out when he wrote, *"that which is not of faith is sin"*, Rom. 14:23.

Again we know these 40 years in the wilderness were normal solar years because nothing to the contrary is mentioned. God had not yet started to use the 360 day year in His calculations regarding punishments.

Applying the year for a day principle to the 2,520 days reveals some very remarkable links between God's judgments against the Jews whilst they were under the Babylonians, and their restoration. I have therefore called the resulting 2,520 solar year period the Babylonian Time Ruler. We find that God only added this Time Ruler to years when Nabopolassar and Nebuchadnezzar came to the throne and ruled Babylon, as these two kings were their most influential ones. The dates of restoration at the other end of the ruler confirm that God has used the solar year for a day principle as part of His calculations.

Even more amazing is that God also took into consideration the Babylonian tradition of calling the year when their new king came to the throne, his "accession" year, whereas the following complete one was referred to as his "first" year. The importance and differentiation between these two years was discovered by archaeologists from clay tablets and papyri, (details in Almost Midnight p105). For instance, King Nabopolassar became king of the new Babylonian Empire in 625 BC, his accession year. The following year, 624 BC, was called his first year. God used him to revive, enlarge and strengthen the empire in readiness for his son Nebuchadnezzar to conquer Jerusalem and defeat the Jews. Add 2,520 years to both these dates and we find they end when God took the first two major steps in restoring the Jewish nation – 1896 when the Jew, Dr. Theodor Herzl, published his book Der Judenstaat (the Jewish State), and the following year, 1897, when he chaired the first International Zionist Conference in Switzerland to discuss how to bring about the establishment of the State of Israel.

Nebopolassar died and Nebuchadnezzar took the throne in 605 BC, his accession year. The latter attacked Jerusalem that same year, removing sovereignty from the Jews and leaving their king, Jehoiakim, in Jerusalem as a vassal monarch. Adding 2,520 years to 605 BC comes to 1916 when the Allied Armies fought the Turks who had ruled the Middle East for over 300 years. This included Palestine, originally named Israel. The Turks had joined the Germans in the First World War. In 1916 Britain and France agreed that once the war had been won, the whole of Palestine should come under British jurisdiction rather than French. It was known as the Sykes-Picot Agreement – another vital and major move in the Jews' restoration. The majority of politicians in the British war cabinet were Bible believing Christians who understood something of what God was doing in restoring the Jews to their historic homeland.

Adding 2,520 years to 604 BC, the "first" year of Nebuchadnezzar, comes to 1917 when the famous Balfour Declaration was drawn up and signed in November by the British Government. This promised to establish a homeland for the Jews. It was similar in magnitude and significance to the decree made by King Cyrus the Great of Persia that the Jews were to return from Babylon to rebuild their Temple in Jerusalem, Ezra 1:1-4. In December of 1917, General Allenby who was Commander of the Allied forces, entered Jerusalem to take it from the defeated Turks. He was a strong Bible-believing man and very aware of the momentous spiritual event taking place. Humbled, he dismounted from his horse and walked in through the city gates in awe of the occasion. He knew his Saviour had previously cried in grief over the Jews' rejection of God's salvation and had ridden in on a colt. Allenby clearly recognized the faithful and almighty hand of God bringing about the restoration of the Jews to the land covenanted to Abraham all those many years before.

The Bible also shows the difference between the "accession" and "first" years. Daniel records King Nebuchadnezzar conquering Jerusalem in what would have been his accession year and *"the third year of Jehoiakim king of Judah"*, Dan. 1:1. But Jeremiah describes *"the fourth year of Jehoiakim, son of Josiah, king of Judah, as the first year of Nebuchadnezzar king of Babylon"*, Jer. 25:1. Before this Babylonian tradition was discovered, critics had jumped on this seeming discrepancy in scripture, but as always the Bible is vindicated once all the facts are known.

Had the Jewish leaders humbled themselves and repented in the first few years of the exile in Babylon, then the more severe "seven times" punishment would not have been implemented, Jerusalem would not have been destroyed and a king could have been restored to the throne at that time. There would have been no need for God to raise up King Cyrus of Persia to conquer the Babylonians and continue Gentile domination over the Jews! Tragically, at every stage they did not repent and so have remained under foreign rulers for the full term of punishment over two millennia.

Now that the Jews have paid for the gross sins committed under the latter period of their kings, God is methodically restoring Israel in our day according to the

law. Again, had they turned to Jesus on a national scale
and accepted Him when He ministered to them 2,000 years
ago or even at any later time, history would have been
very different. However, they have consistently rejected
Him and paid the penalty due to them for both their own
sin and the sins of their predecessors. Praise God, under
the New Covenant, we do not have to pay for the sins of
our forefathers.

One further point is that God did not apply the 2,520 year
Babylonian Time Ruler to 535 BC when the Jews returned to
Jerusalem. This is because the Babylonians were conquered
by King Cyrus in that year, and ceased to have any influence
over the Jews from then onwards.

The Babylonian Time Ruler

625 BC	< 2,520 years >	1896
King Nabopolassar's		Herzl published his
accession year.		book "The Jewish State".

624 BC	< 2,520 years >	1897
His first year.		Herzl chaired the
		First International
		Zionist Conference.

605 BC	< 2,520 years >	1916
King Nebuchadnezzar's		Sykes-Picot decide
accession year.		Britain will govern Palestine.

604 BC	< 2,520 years >	1917
Nebuchadnezzar's		Balfour Declaration.
first year.		General Allenby
		took Jerusalem.

Please persevere with me in all these calculations as it is necessary to understand further how God is working His purposes out through history.

As discussed, God had originally intended just 70 years of foreign rule giving the Jews the opportunity to repent, but they continued to rebel under the Babylonian yolk. Consequently, He then instigated the "seven times" punishment which we have found to be a further 2,520 years. Adding these two periods together totals 2,590 solar years. We have seen that God uses the 360 day year to deduce the lengths of punishment, so if we consider 2,590 solar years in terms of each one only having 360 days, it shortens the total time under judgment to 2,552 solar years (2,590 years divided by 365.25 days x 360 days = 2,552 whole solar years). If this is a correct assumption, it should be the total length of years that foreign powers have governed the Jews since 605 BC and which Jesus described as "*the times of the Gentiles*", *Luke 21:24*. I have called this length of judgment the Gentiles Time Ruler, as it links both periods of punishment to the restoration God is effecting in our day.

Let us see what these correlating years reveal. Adding 2,552 years to 605 BC when Jewish sovereignty was removed, brings us exactly to 1948 when the Jewish State was declared. God gave them back their sovereignty and foreign rule ceased. This is no mere coincidence and far beyond any mathematical chance as it is based on a sound interpretation of Old Testament laws and how God applied them in various situations. The divine Hand has clearly brought it about. The late Derek Prince, a Christian leader of good repute, was living in Jerusalem during the declaration of the State and the immediate attack by the surrounding Muslim nations to try and annihilate her. He said he was very aware of the power of God defending Israel and heard many reports of angelic interventions aiding the Jews during their War of Independence.

I believe this monumental step of the rebirth of Israel and the formation of many other countries following the break-up of the Turkish Empire is what Jesus spoke of when He said, *"look at the fig tree and all the trees. When they sprout leaves, you can see for yourselves and know that summer is near. Even so, when you see these things happening, you know that the kingdom is near"*, *Luke 21:29*. The fig tree always represents Israel. She has been replanted and is once again growing in the right place in the ground of God's choice! The other trees stand for the numerous other nations that have been formed in the Middle East during the last 100 years. Today is truly the Jewish Spring in the Middle East! However, a very hot summer is forecast but is designed to produce a harvest of ripe figs for Jesus to eat in the Autumn. This is speaking of fruitfulness from the Kingdom of God as more and more Jews repent and come to Christ. The Lord says to her:

"See! The winter is past; the rains are over and gone. Flowers appear on the earth; the season of singing has come, the cooing of doves is heard in our land. The fig tree forms its early fruit; the blossoming vines spread their fragrance. Arise, come, my darling; my beautiful one, come with me."

(Song of Songs 2:11-13)

Adding the same Gentiles Time Ruler to 586 BC, when Jerusalem was destroyed and the Jews were taken from the city at the start of the "seven times" judgment, we arrive at 1967 when God restored them back to Jerusalem. This is surely proof positive that it is God who is restoring the Jews both to the land and to their holy city. I believe the years of 1948 and 1967 are the most significant years on the two sloping lines that crossed each other in the vision I was given back in 1977.

Regarding the establishment of the State of Israel in 1948, I cannot overstate the monumental sea change in the spiritual realm that this caused. The Muslims refer to it as "The Catastrophe" because it contradicts what they have been taught i.e. because most of the Jews rebelled against Allah by killing his prophets and changing the scriptures, they must be punished and removed at all costs. This is a diabolical deception, denying Palestinians the enormous blessing of being associated with the Jews' return to the land. Even though they are taught to hate Jews, Jesus is standing in front of them with open arms, drawing them into His welcoming embrace as God wants none to perish. More of them are responding to this love and are coming to Christ. Satan, however, has nowhere to turn and is becoming ever more desperate and angry, throwing everything he can at the Jews. For instance, Ayatollah Ali Khamenei, the supreme leader of Iran and President Ahmadinejad, his current spokesman, have both declared their intention of wiping Israel and her Jewish population off the map. They have publically stated it is their moral duty to carry this out. There are currently nearly six million Jews living in Israel and the Iranian leadership earnestly desires a second Holocaust. This objective is shared by every militant Muslim group around the world but the Lord will deal with them if they do not repent, Ps. 2. The sands of time are running out for Satan.

I said in Almost Midnight, p 132, that God may have added the 2,552 year Ruler to 535 BC at the end of the Babylonian judgment when the Persians took over Israel. If this is so, the corresponding end date comes to 2018 when we would see the third largest change in Israel's restoration after 1948 and 1967. As cautioned in my book, because 2011 has not seen the restoration of Temple sacrifice, which has to happen seven years before the Lord's return, 2018 will not see Jesus coming in all His glory and power.

The Gentiles Time Ruler

605 BC Jewish Sovereignty lost lost to Babylonians.	< 2,522 years >	1948 Jewish Sovereignty regained.
586 BC Jews removed from Jerusalem.	< 2,522 years >	1967 Jews restored to Jerusalem.
535BC Babylonian rule ends. Persians take over Israel.	< 2,522 years >	2018? Third and last major step in the restoration of the Jews?

We will have to wait and see what 2018 brings.

8 *"Time, Times and Half a Time"*

IIIIIIIIIIIIIIIIIIIIIIIIIIIIIIIIIIIIIIIIIIIIIIIIIIIIIIIIIIIIIIIIIIIIIIIIIIIIIIIIIIIIIIIIIIIIIIIIIIIIIIII

In the last chapter, I explained that the word *"time"* in the context of a judgment period means a year of 360 days. The plural *"times"* doubles it making 720 days and *"half a time"* is 180 days – a grand total of 1,260 days. This is three and a half judgment years. The plural "times" cannot mean more than 2 x 360 as a greater multiple does not fit the other scriptures which say the period is 1,260 days, as I will seek to show.

$$
\begin{array}{rcl}
 & & 360 \text{ days} \\
\text{Twice } 360 & = & 720 \text{ days} \\
\text{Half of } 360 & = & \mathbf{180\ days} \\
\hline
 & & 1{,}260 \text{ days}
\end{array}
$$

We can now understand more clearly God's use of this highly unusual phrase to describe a specific period which appears in several places in the Bible. For instance, when Daniel was exiled in Babylon he heard an angel using it to explain how long the saints would suffer violence at the very end of this age:

> *"One of them* (an angel) *said to the man clothed in linen* (another angel)*, who was above the waters of the river,*

"how long will it be before these astonishing things are
fulfilled?" (the end-time wrath of God). *The man clothed*
in linen, who was above the waters of the river, lifted his
right hand and his left hand toward heaven, and I heard
him swear by him who lives forever, saying, "It will be
for a time, times and half a time. When the power of the
holy people has been finally broken, all these things will
be completed."

(Daniel 12:6-7)

The same phrase also appears in Revelation 12 in the New
Testament, where another angel spoke to the apostle John whilst
he was imprisoned on the Isle of Patmos. This whole chapter
gives an overarching vision of the Jewish people as symbolized
by a "woman", and has deliberate similarities to Joseph's vision
of his family bowing down to him, Gen. 37:9-11. Rev. 12:1
shows the "woman" clothed with the sun, the moon is under her
feet and there are 12 stars around her head. Here, as in Joseph's
dream, the sun and moon represent Jacob (renamed Israel) and
Rachel his wife, and the stars are the 12 tribes of Israel. The
"woman" gave birth to a male child, referring to Jesus being
brought forth from the Jewish nation and in particular from
Mary who actually bore Him, Rev. 12:1-5. The next verse says
the child was taken up to heaven, speaking of His ascension,
and then the "woman" was:

"taken care of in the desert for 1,260 days."

(Revelation 12:6)

This respite in the wilderness is speaking of an event
subsequent to the ascension, and since we have not yet seen

the Jews being *"taken care of"*, far from it, this remains in the future. It also shows that the "woman" is not symbolising Mary but the Jewish nation, as she is spoken of as being on earth during the 1,260 day period in the last years of this age. This same length of days is described eight verses later using the same unusual phrase, *"time, times and half a time"*:

> *"The woman* (the Jews) *was given the two wings of a great eagle, so that she might fly to the place prepared for her in the wilderness, where she would be taken care of for a time, times and half a time, out of the serpent's reach. Then from his mouth the serpent spewed water like a river, to overtake the woman and sweep her away with the torrent. But the earth helped the woman by opening its mouth and swallowing the river that the dragon had spewed out of his mouth. Then the dragon was enraged at the woman and went off to make war against the rest of her offspring—those who keep God's commands and hold fast their testimony about Jesus."*
>
> (Revelation 12:14-17)

We also see in the above verses that the dragon is thwarted in spewing out his evil plans against the Jews, so he turns to pursuing Gentiles who are following Jesus.

The appearance of this phrase in the New Testament shows that God continues to use the 360 day year with regard to the Jews. It confirms they are still under some form of Gentile domination until they govern the whole land promised to them, Zech. 14:2. Rejection of their Messiah is delaying their restoration and ensures they are still being judged by the law as a nation.

Interestingly, the protection of the Jews revealed to John in the above passage is exactly the opposite to Daniel's vision where *"the power of the holy people has been finally broken"*, *Daniel 12:7*. Here the angel is clearly describing the Jewish nation as holy in the sense that they remain a special nation separated to God. The Hebrew word "yad" translated "power" in this verse refers to their own strength and not the Lord's. He requires the Jews as a nation to come to the end of their abilities that He might bring them to their Messiah and so accomplish His promises to Abraham. God said to Abraham that He would give them victory over their enemies and make them mighty *"Your descendants will take possession of the cities of their enemies, and through your offspring all nations on earth will be blessed"*, *Gen. 22:17-18*. In our time we have seen this happening since 1948 but there is still much more to do. I am reminded of part of the Song of Moses *"The Lord will judge His people and have compassion on His servants when He sees their strength has gone"*, *Deut. 32:36*.

Being described as holy before they are saved is similar to the unbelieving wife of a believing husband, or vice versa, being considered holy by the Lord, 1 Cor. 7:14. Paul also said *"if the part of the dough offered as first fruits is holy, then the whole batch is holy"*, *Rom. 11:16*. Replacement Theology says that the "holy people" in the above verse only refers to saved Jews and Gentiles, but I believe their interpretation misses the point of what God is doing.

As God uses the 360 day year in the last years before Jesus returns, which, as I have shown in chapter 5, are the last seven years of God's decree over the Jews and Jerusalem, we are now in a position to see that, in God's eyes, each of the 490 years spoken of in the decree are also considered to be

360 days long. I explain this further in chapter 13. This means that in God's calculations the first 483 years reduce down to 476 solar years (483 divided by 365.25 x 360) which brings secular history into a perfect match with the inerrant biblical timing of God's Word. Significantly, also notice that God does not use the word "year" in the Daniel 9:24-27 prophecy, but describes the period as *"seventy sevens"* (seventy weeks). This further points to special judgment years being used in the 490 year prophecy and not normal solar years. I deal with this fully in Almost Midnight.

Again, we will have to wait and see how all these prophecies work out in detail but I believe the Holy Spirit will make everything much clearer as we enter these years. God wants all men to be saved and He has promised to bring the whole remnant of Jews to salvation. He will employ all means possible to bring this about so He can reveal His love, mercy and grace to them.

9 *Prophecies Yet to be Fulfilled*

There are numerous prophecies throughout the Old and New Testaments saying that the Jews would return to Israel at the end of this age. As I have shown from Scripture, we are seeing God bringing His judgments on Israel to an end but Replacement Theology says God has already fulfilled them or cancelled them for disobedience. If it is the latter, He could also do this for promises to believers under the New Covenant for exactly the same reason, as there is not one Christian who is remotely worthy enough in his own right to stand before God.

So, let us look at Zechariah's words more closely to clarify what God has fulfilled, withdrawn or has yet to accomplish. To start with, His judgments on the Jews are coming to an end so if the following prophecy is yet to be fulfilled, the Gentile nations need to take heed because God is once again fighting for Israel:

*"I am going to make Jerusalem a cup that sends all the surrounding people **reeling**. Judah will be besieged as well as Jerusalem. On that day, when all the nations of the earth are gathered against her, I will make Jerusalem an*

immovable rock for all the nations. All who try to move it
*will **injure themselves**."*

(Zechariah 12:2-3)

The Romans under General Titus savagely destroyed
Jerusalem and the surrounding towns in 70 AD without
any insurmountable problems. The empire was not sent
"reeling" so this prophecy could not have been fulfilled
then. Moreover, many powers since then have run
roughshod over the city, but it was a different story in 1948
when the Muslim nations surrounding Israel attacked the
newly born fledgling State (shades of Herod murdering all
the children under two in the area of Bethlehem to try and
stop God's plan through the baby Jesus, Matt. 2:16-18).
During the U.N. vote in 1947 to authorize an Israeli state,
the British government abstained to keep in with the Arabs
because of oil and the Suez Canal. When the last troops
from the British Army pulled out in early May 1948,
they compounded the treachery by not only creating a
vacuum for the militants to bring further violence but
also by leaving the Arabs much of their heavy artillery.
The Muslims were then far better equipped than the Jews
at that extremely critical time.

The U.N. plan was to divide the land so both parties could
have a State, leaving Jerusalem as a separate international
city entirely surrounded by Palestinian territory. Although
it was a bad deal for the Jews, they accepted the U.N. vote
and declared their State in May 1948. The whole idea was
rejected by the Palestinians and the surrounding Arab
nations on religious grounds. The Palestinians wanted the
whole land without a Jew in sight and chose annihilation

of the new born state. Most governments thought that Israel would not last two weeks but, on the contrary, she gained more ground than originally allocated! The Arabs were therefore the first to come unstuck and they *"injured themselves"*. This is because the times of the Gentiles are in the process of being completed and Israel had been given back sovereignty as a first step in her restoration. Zechariah's prophecy is beginning to be fulfilled in our day!

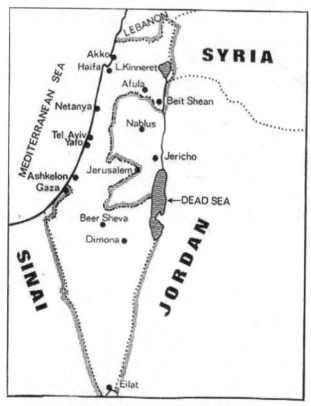

After 1948/49 War of Independence

A similar miracle of expansion happened in 1967 when President Nasser of Egypt ordered the UN buffer peace keeping force to leave his Sinai border with Israel, saying over Cairo radio that he would annihilate the Jewish State. Through his belligerence he lost the Sinai and Gaza. Jordan and Syria simultaneously attacked Israel and they lost old Jerusalem, the West Bank and more of the Golan Heights. Again, angels were seen intervening for Israel during this war. The West Bank and Gaza had been illegally annexed by the Jordanians and the Egyptians respectively, after the 1948 War of Independence.

We are at the early stages of God bringing all the surrounding nations against Jerusalem, as prophesied in Zech. 12:3 and 14:2. In the process He will show the might of His holy arm in saving Israel from her enemies and bringing her to Himself through faith in Christ:

> *"I will display my glory among the nations, and all the*
> *nations will see the punishment I inflict and the hand I lay*
> *on them. From that day forward the people of Israel will*
> *know that I am the LORD their God."*
>
> (Ezekiel 39:21-22)

Zechariah adds:

> *"On that day I will set out to destroy all the nations that*
> *attack Jerusalem. And I will pour out on the house of*
> *David and the inhabitants of Jerusalem a spirit of grace*
> *and supplication. They will look on me* (Jesus), *the one*
> *they have pierced, and they will mourn for him* (Jesus)
> *as one mourns for an only child, and grieve bitterly for*
> *him as one grieves for a firstborn son. On that day the*

*weeping in Jerusalem will be great, like the weeping
of Hadad Rimmon in the plain of Megiddo.* **The land
will mourn, each clan by itself, with their wives by
themselves: the clan of the house of David and their
wives, the clan of the house of Nathan and their wives,
the clan of the house of Levi and their wives, the clan
of Shimei and their wives, and all the rest of the clans
and their wives. "**

(Zechariah 12:9-14)

He says a spirit of grace and supplication will be poured out
on every inhabitant of Jerusalem, and the whole country will
respond to the Holy Spirit in true repentance. Every family
in each tribe throughout the land will mourn when they
see that it was Jesus their Messiah whom they crucified,
Zech.12:10-12. This national awakening did not happen in
Jerusalem after Jesus died on the cross. Although 3,000 souls
came to the Lord at Pentecost with many more thousands
over the ensuing days, months and years, it was nothing like
a comprehensive repentance of all the people, as described
by Zechariah. He foresaw a national conversion in the end-
times. The apostle Paul was also shown this same destiny
for his people which he described as "... *all Israel will be
saved"*, Rom. 11:26.

Also, we have not yet seen Jesus *"standing on the Mount
of Olives"* when it splits in two, Zech. 14:4, or God sending
a plague on all His enemies, Zech. 14:12-15. Neither of these
occurred when the Romans attacked Jerusalem in 70 AD.

"This is the plague with which the LORD *will strike all the
nations that fought against Jerusalem: Their flesh will rot*

*while they are still standing on their feet, their eyes will rot
in their sockets, and their tongues will rot in their mouths."*

(Zechariah 14:12)

The book of Revelation warns us of even further horrors,
culminating with the seven angels each pouring out bowls of
plagues onto the earth, Rev. 15:6.

Zechariah 14:16 then looks even further forward to the
Millennium, the 1,000 year reign of Jesus on earth. By then,
the remnant of the Jewish nation will have come to Christ and
the Holy Spirit will reveal to them that Jesus has fulfilled the
feasts in their entirety. All people will be able to relate with
Jesus in person in Israel during the Millennium rather than
just experience the rituals of the law which are only shadows.
According to Zechariah, Gentile believers will live in their
own native countries and go to worship Jesus. I believe this
will be both awesome and paradoxically very relaxed, just
as Adam walked with God in the garden in the cool of the
evening and when Jesus cooked breakfast for His disciples on
one occasion after His resurrection.

*"Then the survivors from all the nations that have
attacked Jerusalem will go up year after year to worship
the King, the Lord God Almighty, and to celebrate the
Feast of Tabernacles."*

(Zechariah 14:16)

The tabernacles, or shelters, made of leafy branches, were
to remind the Jews of their temporary dwellings in the
wilderness after God delivered them from slavery in Egypt.
Jesus fulfilled this symbolism by tabernacling with the Jews

in His temporary natural body for 33 years in the spiritual wilderness of Israel, as John pointed out when he wrote *"Jesus made His dwelling* (Greek tabernacle) *amongst us," John 1:14.* Praise God, He is now in His permanent eternal resurrection body! The feast was also a picture of the Church today in the spiritual wilderness of this world. We are currently pilgrims here on earth, 1 Pet. 2:11, until we too receive our own permanent resurrection bodies and reign with Jesus in the Millennium! Because Tabernacles was in late summer to celebrate the harvest for that year, it also represents the celebration for the harvest of every precious soul that Jesus will have saved from the bondage of sin (Egypt) throughout the Church age. All these aspects are integrated in this feast but the main one is to point us to our fellowship with Jesus forever.

There is one isolated verse, Zech.13:7, which does not follow the time narrative of these last years in the rest of the chapter, and is clearly a prophetic insight regarding the scattering of Jesus' disciples after His crucifixion. Jesus actually quoted this verse to His disciples in the garden of Gethsemane on the Mount of Olives just before He prayed and was then arrested by the High Priest and elders, Matt. 26:31.

"7Awake, sword, against my shepherd, against the man who is close to me!" declares the LORD Almighty. "Strike the shepherd, and the sheep will be scattered, and I will turn my hand against the little ones.

8In the whole land," declares the LORD, "two-thirds will be struck down and perish; yet one-third will be left in it.

9This third I will bring into the fire; I will refine them like silver and test them like gold. They will call on my

name and I will answer them; I will say, 'They are my
people, and they will say, 'The LORD is our God.'"

(Zechariah 13:7-9)

At first glance, verses 8 and 9 seem to continue on from
verse 7, but on further inspection they are speaking of
the same end-time events of verses 1 to 6 earlier in the
chapter. They prophesy that one third of the survivors
who remain in the land will call on the name of the Lord
which, since the crucifixion, means calling on the name
of Jesus. In 70 AD, one third of the Jews did not remain
in the land and come to Jesus to be refined in the fire.
On the contrary, when the Messianic Jews saw Jerusalem
surrounded by armies, which was a further step in the
Leviticus 26:25 judgment, they escaped from Jerusalem
in obedience to Jesus' instructions to flee, Luke 21:20-24.
Those who rejected Christ, but were not slaughtered
by Titus, either fled to safety or were taken as slaves
to distant parts of the Roman Empire. Some have even
thought this prophecy referred to Hitler's Nazi death
camps, but his industrial murder factories were not in
Israel as the prophecy requires. So, here again, apart from
verse 7, nothing matches history so far.

Clearly chapters 12, 13 and 14 of Zechariah bear no relation
to what transpired when the Romans destroyed Jerusalem
in 70 AD. But, we **are** seeing chapter 12 coming to pass in
our day with the reversal of Israel's military fortunes and an
increasing number of Jews receiving their Messiah, Jesus.
One day soon, all three of these chapters will be completely
fulfilled and Jesus will have made His glorious entry to

Jerusalem after standing once again on the Mount of Olives, Zech. 14:14.

On the subject of the "catching up" (the rapture) of the Church, the Bible only ever uses the expression *"fallen asleep"* for believers who have physically died, as they leave their bodies behind, giving the appearance of sleeping. This phrase is never used to describe those who are raptured, for they will never physically die! Instead, their natural bodies will be transformed into resurrection bodies and be immediately lifted up to meet Jesus in the clouds at His return. The following passage makes it very clear that it is those who have fallen asleep who return with Jesus from heaven at the end of the Tribulation. All three verses highlighted below only refer to these Christians who have died during the Church age and not raptured believers:

*"[13]Brothers and sisters, we do not want you to be uninformed about those who **sleep in death**, so that you do not grieve like the rest, who have no hope.*

*[14]We believe that Jesus died and rose again, and so we believe that God will bring with Jesus those who have fallen **asleep in him**.*

[15]According to the Lord's word, we tell you that we who are still alive, who are left till the coming of the Lord, will certainly not precede those who have fallen asleep.

*[16] For the Lord himself will come down from heaven, with a loud command, with the voice of the archangel and with the trumpet call of God (the last trumpet), and **the dead in Christ will rise first**.*

> [17]*After that, we who are still alive and are left will be*
> *caught up together with them in the clouds to meet the*
> *Lord in the air. And so we will be with the Lord forever."*
> (1 Thessalonians 4:13-17)

On His return, Jesus tarries in the air with believers who have physically died in faith and whose spirits have been in heaven with Him. At that point they will receive their resurrection bodies, which Paul describes as *"the dead in Christ will rise first"*. Despite their spirits being with Him, I believe this phraseology is used by Paul because he sees their dead bodies being figuratively raised from the grave. While they are in the clouds, the angels are gathering up believers who are still alive from around the earth, Matt. 24:30-31. These raptured Christians then have their physical bodies transformed "in the twinkling of an eye", 1 Cor. 15:52, and are taken up to meet Jesus and the others in the air. Neither He nor Paul, nor anyone else in the Bible, ever mentions a secret return to "catch up" believers at the start of the End-time Tribulation!

Once both groups of believers have met together in their resurrection bodies in the clouds, it is there that the *"wedding of the Lamb takes place"*. This is followed by *"the wedding supper of the Lamb"*, Rev. 19:6-9, away from the world where the rebellion on earth is reaching its diabolical fullness. Indeed, this is the whole reason for the rapture, so the Church has no contact or disturbance from the Antichrist and his followers down on the earth whilst the wedding is in progress. It is not stated how long the proceedings will last but it's going to be the most amazing wedding ever held!

Then Jesus and His angels, not the Church, will set to work dealing with all those on earth who have the Mark of the Beast, resulting in the "great supper of God". Thankfully, this and the supper of the Lamb are two different events!

"And I saw an angel standing in the sun, who cried in a loud voice to all the birds flying in midair, "Come, gather together for the great supper of God, so that you may eat the flesh of kings, generals, and the mighty, of horses and their riders, and the flesh of all people, free and slave, great and small. Then I saw the beast and the kings of the earth and their armies gathered together to wage war against the rider on the horse and his army. But the beast was captured, and with it the false prophet who had performed the signs on its behalf. With these signs he had deluded those who had received the mark of the beast and worshiped its image. The two of them were thrown alive into the fiery lake of burning sulphur. The rest were killed with the sword coming out of the mouth of the rider on the horse, and all the birds gorged themselves on their flesh."

(Revelation 19:17-21)

Physical peace then comes to the whole earth in readiness for the glorious 1,000 year reign of Jesus who will bring His new wife, the Church, with Him! Jesus will be in absolute charge and any promises still outstanding to the Jews will be fulfilled.

Some pre-Tribulation believers have thought that when Jesus said, "I will come like a thief in night", He was speaking to the Church but He was actually referring to unbelievers and

Christians who are not walking with Him and therefore will be taken by surprise at His appearance, Rev. 3:3. He was not meaning a secret return that would happen at some unspecified time before the wrath of God is unleashed on the earth. Paul had explained these end-time events to the Thessalonians when he was with them and clarified some of the points in his letter, but the Church has become very confused on the timing of the "catching up" since then.

> *"Now, brothers and sisters, about times and dates we do not need to write to you, for you know very well that the day of the Lord will come like a thief in the night. While people are saying, "Peace and safety," destruction will come on them suddenly, as labour pains on a pregnant woman, and they will not escape.*
>
> *But you, brothers and sisters, are not in darkness so that this day should surprise you like a thief. You are all children of the light and children of the day. We do not belong to the night or to the darkness. So then, let us not be like others, who are asleep, but let us be awake and sober."*
>
> (1 Thessalonians 5:1-6)

The Holy Spirit is once again giving revelation on these teachings so the Church does not remain in darkness.

Also, Revelation 19 says, *"the bride has made herself ready. Fine linen was given her to wear. (Fine linen stands for the righteous acts of the saints.)"*, Rev. 19:7-8. The Church cannot make herself ready in heaven as righteous acts only refer to good deeds done on earth. As she remains here through these years, she will demonstrate her true love for the Bridegroom by laying her life down for Him and others. These verses do not support a pre-Tribulation rapture.

Furthermore, we read *"The Spirit and the bride say"come""*, *Rev. 22:17*. This is not addressed to Jesus, the Bridegroom, but to the lost who are being encouraged to come and drink of the water of life. If the whole Church, the bride, was in heaven "making herself ready" she could not speak to the lost on the earth. The verse is not to be confused with the penultimate one in Revelation which says "come, Lord Jesus", Rev. 22:20, where the Apostle John **is** speaking to Jesus, who is in heaven. All these scriptures point to the Church remaining on earth until Jesus appears in magnificent glory – the Bridegroom of bridegrooms.

A vital practical point is that if the Church was raptured before the Tribulation, Satan would make mincemeat of those who come to the Lord in the End-time traumas. Cults such as Jehovah Witnesses, Mormons as well as Muslims, Hindus etc., would have a heyday in confusing new believers. God has been carefully dealing with the true Church, bringing more maturity and discernment, ready for her to go through the very exacting time of the Tribulation. New converts can then be prayed for and nurtured.

Some have queried why chapters 6 to 19 of Revelation do not mention very much about the Church. It is because they are mainly concentrating on God's wrath against man's rebellion during the last years of this age. God said everything He needed to say about the Church in chapters 2 and 3, where He encouraged and admonished seven of the many recognized congregations at the time regarding their activities and attitudes for believers down through the centuries. In chapters 6 to 19, He only highlights the 144,000 Jews who come to Christ and

are added to the Church. As we know, the whole remnant of
Jews finally believe and repent but these 12,000 from each
tribe choose to remain celibate and dedicate themselves to
God in a truly remarkable way. Although the saints, both Jew
and Gentile, will be persecuted, history shows this will only
result in many more being added to the Church.

Unfortunately, before all the peace and calm of the
Millennium can happen, the Jews will have to go through
further traumatic events because even today most still reject
Jesus. This awful period called The Time of Jacob's Trouble
is yet to come, Jer. 30:7, and will be the greatest distress
they have ever experienced on the earth, never to be repeated
according to Matthew 24:21. The judgment is designed to cause
the Jews to humble themselves, to become willing listeners to
God both individually and as a nation, and so receive their
Messiah, Jesus. These End-time trials are also intended to
take the world out of its complacency and bring multitudes to
Christ. Although God calls the Jews a stiff-necked people, He
promised the patriarchs He would save them, and as the Holy
Spirit works in their hearts, He will bring about the essential
godly sorrow which leads to repentance.

10 Further Issues Regarding the Land of Israel

There are further points of confusion in Replacement Theology which need addressing. It says, quite rightly, that many things in the Mosaic law are shadows of the realities which are experienced in Christ, Heb.10:1 and that the law, along with its feasts, has been entirely fulfilled by Jesus. However, it erroneously applies the same reasoning to the land which was given to Abraham under an entirely different and previous covenant. It concludes that somehow the land was fulfilled by Jesus and so the Jews no longer have any claim to it. They would say that the Jews have no scriptural basis for being there today.

Firstly, the land is not a shadow and secondly, just as the Mosaic law did not remove any promises from the Abrahamic covenant, so the New Covenant does not either. The whole point of Jesus' ministry and work was to fulfil the law and deal with the sin problem so that the Abrahamic Covenant might come in all its fullness, Gen. 22:18. He started by ministering in the power of the Spirit, first to the Jews and then to the nations through the Church. He never fulfilled the land because the land cannot be fulfilled, only lived in. It does, however, picture the Kingdom but it is not the Kingdom itself.

Importantly, although the land was covenanted to Abraham and his descendants, Gen. 15:18, it actually remains the Lord's and the Israelites are tenants, *"the land is mine and you are but aliens and tenants"*, *Lev.25:23-24*. Similarly, the whole world is the Lord's and all that is in it, Ps. 24:1, but He has given mankind authority to rule over and subdue it. Even though God owns the whole planet, He will not overrule the individual's freewill or disregard the sovereign right of a nation. For instance, He had to obtain Pharaoh's permission to lead the Jews out of Egypt! He also had to wait for the sins of the Amorites to come to the point where judgment was the only remedy for their disobedience. In their case, death and forfeiture of their land:

> *"In the fourth generation your descendants will come*
> *back here, for the sin of the Amorites has not yet reached*
> *its full measure."*
>
> (Genesis 15:16)

In due course God was then able to take control of the promised territories and give them to the Israelites who would be tenants. In the same way, God is tarrying in sending Jesus back because the sins of the whole world have not yet reached their fullness, when judgment will take place. In the meantime He is looking to save as many people as possible before then. The same punishment that Joshua was commanded to carry out against the Canaanites, Amorites etc. will be applied by Jesus, when He returns, to everyone on the face of the earth who has received the Mark of the Beast, Rev.19:21. It must be emphasised that it was because of their gross sin that these nations in Canaan lost their lives and their territories and *"not because of the righteousness of the Israelites"*, *Deut. 9:1-6.* So it will be for the Christians who inherit the earth, for Paul says *"it is by grace you have been saved, through faith – and this not from yourselves, it is the gift of God – not by works, so no-one can boast"*, *Eph. 2:8-9.* Just as the Israelites were given the land, so Christians will be given their own national lands to govern, Zech. 14:16-19.

One of the claims made by Replacement Theology is that the land is not mentioned in the New Testament once the Jews had been expelled from the land. However, this is not correct as there are a number of references to the Jews being in Jerusalem in the book of Revelation. Here, John speaks of temple worship in the city in the end time, Rev. 11:1-13, and the Two Witnesses, probably Moses and Elijah, are shown to be prophesying in Jerusalem then, Rev. 11:8. We have also looked in detail at the words of Jesus when He said *"Jerusalem shall be trampled on until the times of the Gentiles are fulfilled"*, *Luke 21:24*, which effectively states that the Jews will be back in the land. All these scriptures refer to the end of this age when Jerusalem will finally be under Jewish jurisdiction. The apostles taught that all doctrine should be tested and judged against the Old Testament scriptures. If it disagrees, it must be rejected. There is no indication whatsoever that the land will be taken from the Jews and so Replacement Theology must therefore be rejected. The scriptures are overflowing with passages about the Jews being gathered back to the land for a second time in the end days, as well as their on-going presence there in the Millennium, Isaiah 11:11 etc.

Furthermore, Paul in the New Testament saw that the promises spoken to Abraham were actually speaking of Jesus.

"The promises were spoken to Abraham and to his seed.
The scripture does not say "and to seeds" meaning many
*people, but "**and to your seed**" (Gen. 22:18), **meaning***
one person, who is Christ."

(Galatians 3:16)

Jesus has inherited the land from His Father, who was the Landlord. The Jews remain tenants. Very importantly, Gentile believers do not inherit the land as they are only spiritual sons of Abraham through faith in Christ, and not physical sons.

Replacement Theology applies the same reasoning to the land as it does to circumcision. It says, quite rightly, that because physical circumcision is no longer required of the Jew in Christ, so the land is no longer an issue since the New Covenant was introduced. The Holy Spirit does indeed accomplish circumcision of our hearts by crucifying us with Christ at the new birth, Gal. 2:20, so there is no requirement for the Messianic Jew to be physically circumcised. However, there is no parallel with land which cannot be fulfilled.

Now that the punishment of the Jewish nation is drawing to an end and the Lord is bringing the Jews back, those who come against them and divide the land will find themselves coming against **God Himself.** So Church and nations be warned!

"In those days and at that time (at the end of the age
i.e. now), *when I restore the fortunes of Judah and*
Jerusalem I will gather all nations and bring them down

to the Valley of Jehoshaphat (Armageddon). *There I will
enter into judgment against them* (the Gentiles that attack
the Jews) *concerning my inheritance, my people Israel, for
they scattered my people among the nations and divided
up my land."*

(Joel 3:1-3)

As we have seen, Israel's military fortunes have changed
since 1948 due to God removing some of His punishments
from the nation. Just as He increased them in steps, so He is
in the process of removing them in steps. He is once again
fighting for the Jews to regain the land as long as they do not
agree to give it up. When the Israeli government handed Gaza
over in the hope of peace, all they received in return were
rockets, bringing more death and destruction. Since 1948,
Satan needs the Jews' permission to take their land. So he
is therefore applying extreme political pressure against them
through the politicians, as well as terrorism etc, cleverly
using lies and deception to make Israel out to be the villain of
the piece in the world's eyes. The Jews are far from perfect
and act in many wrong ways, but nothing on the scale of
Muslim fundamentalists who attack and kill Jewish families
with young children, as well as their own people in Gaza and
around the world, all indiscriminately and without mercy!
The active terrorists purposely hide amongst their own wives
and children, being willing to sacrifice them for shocking
headlines and political gain. When invading Gaza, the Israeli
Defense Force leafleted the areas where they intended to
attack, but many Palestinian women and children remained
in the firing line, gaining sympathy from the outside world
when they were wounded or killed. Contrary to the Oslo

Accords which stipulate that both governments be actively committed to peace building, Palestinian schoolchildren are taught to hate the Jews and some are even instructed on how to blow them up, killing themselves in the process as an act of so called heroism. The spirit of child sacrifice lives on in modern guise.

Since it is God who is restoring the Jews to the land, it is desperately serious that the world and the Church do not go against His will and force a Two State Solution. We need to earnestly pray that this will not happen. As the previous quote shows, Joel gives a strong warning that God will deal very severely with any nation that divides the land of Israel.

There is a prophecy in Ezekiel 36 which deserves special mention. It gives specific insights into the importance of the land to God, especially its mountains, and provides further explanation as to what He is in the process of bringing about today. The relevant scriptures are:

Ezekiel 36:
  Verses 3-6
  "³Therefore prophesy and say, 'This is what the
  Sovereign LORD says: Because they ravaged and hounded
  you from every side so that you (the mountains) ***became***
  ***the possession of the rest of the nations** and the object of*
  people's malicious talk and slander,
    ⁴therefore, O mountains of Israel, hear the word of the
  Sovereign LORD: This is what the Sovereign LORD says
  to the mountains and hills, to the ravines and valleys,
  to the desolate ruins and the deserted towns that have
  been plundered and ridiculed by the rest of the nations
  around you.

> *⁵this is what the Sovereign LORD says: In my burning
> zeal I have spoken against the rest of the nations, and
> against all **Edom**, for with glee and with malice in their
> hearts they made my land their own possession so that
> they might plunder its pastureland.'*
>
> *⁶Therefore prophesy concerning the land of Israel
> and say to the mountains and hills, to the ravines and
> valleys: 'This is what the Sovereign LORD says: I speak in
> my jealous wrath because you have suffered the scorn of
> the nations."*

The judgment against Edom, verse 5, has already taken place
as it is a largely deserted and desolate place with only the
tourist attraction of Petra remaining.

Verse 12
> *"I will cause people, my people Israel, to walk upon
> you* (the mountains of Israel). *They will posses you, and
> you will be their inheritance; **you will never deprive them
> again of their children.**"*

Please note here that God says He will bring the Israelites
back to the mountains of Israel, meaning the mountains of
Judea and Samaria, which is more or less the same area today
described as the West Bank.

As investigated in depth, Jesus warned the Jews of a second
expulsion from the land when He said, *"They* (the Jews) *will fall
by the sword and will be taken as prisoners to all the nations.
Jerusalem will* (continue to) *be trampled on by the Gentiles until
the times of the Gentiles are fulfilled", Luke 21:20-24.* Therefore,
when Ezekiel wrote in verse 12 that *"you* (the mountains) *will*

never deprive them (the Jews) *again of their children"* he could not have been speaking about the first restoration from Babylon in 535 BC, as they were to be separated from the mountains a second time by the Romans in 70 AD. Since there are only two dispersions and returns prophesied in the Bible, the ingathering we are seeing today must be the second and last one.

Verses 22-28

"²²Therefore say to the house of Israel, thus says the Lord God, "it is not for your sake O house of Israel, that I am about to act but for My Holy name, which you have profaned among the nations where you went.

²³I will vindicate the holiness of my great name which has been profaned among the nations, the name which you have profaned in their midst. **Then the nations will know that I am the Lord", declares the Lord God, "when I prove Myself holy among you in their sight.**

²⁴For I will take you from the nations, gather you from all the lands and bring you back into your own land.

²⁵I will sprinkle clean water on you, and you will be clean; I will cleanse you from your impurities and from all your idols.

²⁶I will give you a new heart and put a new spirit in you (the new birth in Christ) *I will remove from you your heart of stone and give you a heart of flesh.*

²⁷And I will put my Spirit in you and move you to follow all my decrees and be careful to keep my laws (now the law of Christ, 1 Cor. 9:20).

²⁸You will live in the land I gave; you will be my people, and I will be your God."

(Ezekiel 36:22-28)

Verse 23 gives a clear warning to the governments of the world that God is preparing to reveal His holiness through an awesome display of power in establishing the Jews in the whole land, and bringing them into relationship with Himself through Christ.

Through the vision of "the valley of dry bones", Ezekiel prophesies that the ten northern tribes and two southern tribes will be re-united and brought back to the land under the reign of their King, who we now know to be Jesus, their Messiah. This prophecy was given hundreds of years after King David was on the throne:

> *"This is what the Sovereign LORD says: I am going to take the stick of Joseph—which is in Ephraim's hand—and of the Israelite tribes associated with him, and join it to Judah's stick. I will make them into a single stick of wood, and they will become one in my hand. Hold before their eyes the sticks you have written on and say to them, 'This is what the Sovereign LORD says: I will take the Israelites out of the nations where they have gone. I will gather them from all around and bring them back into their own land. I will make them one nation in the land, on the mountains of Israel.' There will be one king over all of them and they will never again be two nations or be divided into two kingdoms. They will no longer defile themselves with their idols and vile images or with any of their offenses, for I will save them from all their sinful backsliding, and I will cleanse them. They will be my people, and I will be their God. My servant David* (King Jesus) *will be king over them, and they will all have one shepherd. They will follow my laws* (now laws in Christ) *and be careful to keep my*

*decrees. They will live in the land I gave to my servant
Jacob, the land where your ancestors lived. They and
their children and their children's children will live there
forever, and David my servant will be their prince forever.
I will make a covenant of peace with them* (the New
Covenant); *it will be an everlasting covenant. I will
establish them and increase their numbers, and I will put
my sanctuary among them forever. My dwelling place will
be with them; I will be their God, and they will be my
people. Then the nations will know that I the* LORD *make
Israel holy, when my sanctuary is among them forever.'"*

(Ezekiel 37:19-28)

From heaps of bones in the Nazi death camps there is now a
vibrant nation with an ever increasing number of Jews coming
to Christ. We are starting to see these events happen. May I
suggest you read the whole of chapters 36, 37, 38 and 39 of
Ezekiel, as all of the prophecies will be totally fulfilled before
too long.

Since 1896, through the publication of Der Judenstaat
(The Jewish State) by the socialist Dr. Theodor Herzl, God
initiated His plan of restoration for Israel, which meant a
marked increase in the number of Jews returning to the
land. Satan responded to the situation by bringing large
numbers of Muslims into Israel, particularly from Jordan,
specifically designed to counter God's purposes. We should
not be surprised at this type of manipulation of people as John
says, *"the whole world is under the control of the Evil One",
1 John 5:19.* Satan is out to oppose God solely to save himself.
His pawns include both the poor Palestinian citizens as well
as their leaders, who are being deceived into waging endless

conflicts and wars against Israel. We must earnestly pray and have compassion on them as well as the Jews. Just as there were many good, caring German families during the Second World War, so there are many good, upright Palestinian families caught in Satan's deceptions.

If one ignores God's Word, it would seem sensible to trade land for peace, but God will not change any covenant He has made, especially with an assembly of unrighteous nations called the U.N. who are in open rebellion to Him. Yitzhak Rabin, a secular rather than a Messianic Jew, bowed to pressure and recognized the Palestinian National Authority at the Oslo Peace Accords in 1993, hoping for reconciliation – land for peace. This foolish policy has opened the door to a possible Palestinian State in the land of Israel and has also set the U.N. on a collision course with God.

For those who have eyes to see, there is an enormous spiritual battle raging for the Promised Land and we must continue to pray for God's mercy and for His Word to be accomplished. Satan knows only too well that God has promised to bring the Jews back before Jesus returns, Ezek. 36:8-24, and give them a new heart through faith in their Messiah, Ezek. 36:25-27. Satan is delighted with Replacement Theology which has no doctrinal problem with a Two-State Solution or even the total removal of Jews from the land. If he can stop them possessing the promised territory, he can stop the return of Jesus and thus avoid being thrown into prison (the Abyss) during the Millennium, Rev. 20:1-3. His further prospects are even worse – eternity in the lake of fire, Rev. 20:10.

Whilst considering Ezekiel's prophecies, it is worth mentioning his detailed visions of the temple, as recorded in chapters 40-48. It is vital to see that Jesus became the sin offering for all people who have lived on this planet and fulfilled every aspect of the many sacrifices made by the Levitical priesthood. Jesus opened the new and living way into the Father's presence through His blood, Heb. 10:20-23, and became the perfect High Priest before the Father. God tore the curtain in the Temple from top to bottom the moment Jesus died, Matt.27:50-51 and Heb.10:19-29, signifying the end of the Levitical priesthood. Consequently, the Levites who were to administer the sacrificial system in Ezekiel's temple, Ezek. 44:10-31, have been superseded by the royal priesthood in Christ. Jesus was descended by birth from the tribe of Judah and not Levi, Heb. 7 and 8. This change of priesthood makes Ezekiel's temple redundant, as confirmed by the book of Revelation where there is no sign of a Temple or sacrifice being continued into either the Millennium or on the New Earth. But no doubt the Antichrist will use the ignorance of the Jews about this to fool the religious people into building a Solomon type temple with the Levites ministering once again.

There is no scriptural problem with the land being allocated to the Jews during the Millennium as detailed in Ezekiel chapters 47-48, but here again we shall have to wait and see what transpires.

11 *The Boundaries of the Promised Land*

The Jews are destined, at some point, to possess all the territories promised by God to Abraham and his descendants. Since 1948, they have gained ground each time the Arabs have attacked, so it may well be that the next big attack by the surrounding Muslim nations will see more ground, if not all the remainder being taken. So, what land will these boundaries include? The following scripture provides details:

> *"When the sun had set and darkness had fallen, a smoking firepot with a blazing torch appeared and passed between the pieces. On that day the* LORD *made a covenant with Abram and said, "To your descendants I give this land, from the Wadi of Egypt* (the border with Egypt) *up to the great river, the Euphrates— the land of the Kenites, Kenizzites, Kadmonite, Hittites, Perizzites, Rephaites, Amorites, Canaanites,Girgashites and Jebusites."*

(Genesis15:17-21)

Very significantly, when we were praying for Israel in April 2011, one of our prayer partners had a vision of a flaming brazier which we believe was God confirming to us that He has not forgotten His covenant with Abraham regarding the land. At the time, she was new to praying for Israel and was unaware of the vision given to Abraham of God walking through the severed pieces of the sacrifice.

The following map clarifies the land inheritance promised to Abraham:

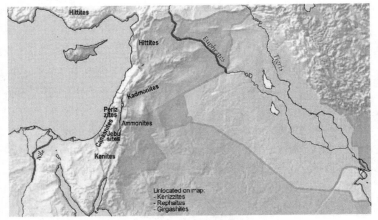

The extent of the Promised Land, Genesis 15:17-21

The two most startling future additions to territory, not yet considered in the present impasse between the Israelis and the Palestinians, are those of the Hittites and the Kadmonites. As can be seen from the map, the Hittite empire extended down to the northern half of present day Syria. The Kadmonites were in the southern part of Syria, stretching into Lebanon. We know that the land of the Amorites to the east of the Jordan River was part of the land of Israel during the time of Jesus on earth. It was included in the Ammonite territories, as per the above map, which was a general name for the eastern peoples. Matthew records that people from the Decapolis (ten major towns to the east of Lake Galilee and the River Jordan) came to hear Him, Matt. 4:25. His ministry was only to the Jews in Israel, so these areas were part of the Promised Land as well.

So let us see how much of the land was successfully possessed by the Jews in those early days when they first entered the land. Moses took the Amorite territory, which they named Gilead. He granted the request of the two and a half tribes who wanted to live there, provided they sent their fighting men to aid their brother Israelites in possessing the land on the west side of the River Jordan, Num. 32. They could then return to Gilead. Joshua succeeded Moses, crossed the River Jordan and took much more of the promised territory, but large areas were still left to be possessed.

"When Joshua had grown old, the LORD said to him, "You are now very old, and there are still very large areas of land to be taken over."

(Joshua 13:1)

"This is the land that remains: all the regions of the Philistines and Geshurites, from the Shihor River on the east of Egypt (on the border) *to the territory of Ekron on the north, all of it counted as Canaanite though held by the five Philistine rulers in Gaza, Ashdod, Ashkelon, Gath and Ekron* (all this covers the Gaza strip from the border with Egypt – which was probably the Wadi of Egypt)*; the territory of the Avvites on the south* (northern Negev, south east of Gaza)*; all the land of the Canaanites, from Arah of the Sidonians* (north of present day Israel) *as far as Aphek*

and the border of the Amorites, (that lay on the eastern
side of the Jordan); *the area of Byblos* (West coast port,
north of Beirut in Lebanon); *and all Lebanon to the east,
from Baal Gad below Mount Hermon to Lebo Hamath*
(north of Damascus up to the Euphrates).

   *As for all the inhabitants of the mountain regions from
Lebanon to Misrephoth Maim* (near Sidon), *that is, all the
Sidonians, I myself* (Joshua) *will drive them out before
the Israelites. Be sure to allocate this land to Israel for
an inheritance, as I have instructed you, and divide it as
an inheritance among the nine tribes and half of the tribe
of Manasseh."*

(Joshua 13:2-7)

It was left to King David to take the remaining territories
untouched by Joshua but promised to Abraham, and to
complete God's judgment against child sacrifice, temple
prostitution etc. which was being practised in all these lands.

   The following map and scriptures show the final extent of
the kingdom. The prophet Samuel records how David finished
the task and took all the land up to the Euphrates, north east of
Damascus. Ammon (east of the River Jordan, where the present
day city of Amman is situated) had already been taken by Moses
and renamed Gilead. David secured Moab (south of Ammon
and east of the Dead Sea) and Edom (below Moab). After many
years of fighting with the likes of Goliath, he eventually took the
land of the Philistines, to the south west of central Israel (Gaza)
and that of the Amalek people to the south of Israel. However,
like Joshua he did not kill all the inhabitants of the newly gained
territories as God had commanded. They have consequently
been a thorn in Israel's side ever since, Deut. 7:1-9:

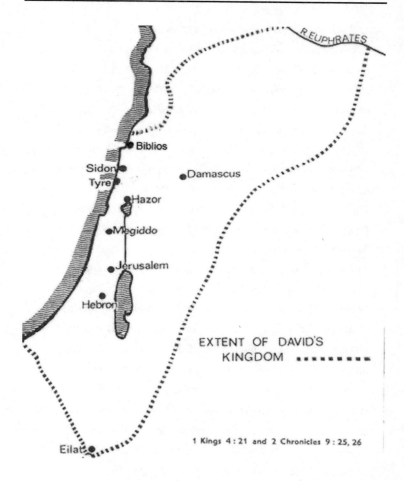

R EUPHRATES

Biblios

Sidon
Tyre

●Damascus

●Hazor

●Megiddo

●Jerusalem

Hebron

EXTENT OF DAVID'S
KINGDOM ■ ■ ■ ■ ■ ■ ■ ■

1 Kings 4 : 21 and 2 Chronicles 9 : 25, 26

Eilat

*"In the course of time, David defeated the Philistines
and subdued them, and he took Metheg Ammah from
the control of the Philistines. David also defeated the
Moabites. He made them lie down on the ground and
measured them off with a length of cord. Every two
lengths of them were put to death, and the third length was
allowed to live. So the Moabites became subject to David
and brought him tribute.*

Moreover, David defeated Hadadezer son of Rehob,
king of Zobah (Syria, up to the River Euphrates), *when*
he went to restore his monument at the Euphrates
River. David captured a thousand of his chariots, seven
thousand charioteers and twenty thousand foot soldiers.
He hamstrung all but a hundred of the chariot horses.
When the Arameans of Damascus came to help Hadadezer
king of Zobah, David struck down twenty-two thousand
of them. He put garrisons in the Aramean kingdom of
Damascus, and the Arameans became subject to him and
brought tribute. The LORD *gave David victory wherever*
he went. David took the gold shields that belonged to the
officers of Hadadezer and brought them to Jerusalem.
From Tebah and Berothai, towns that belonged to
Hadadezer, King David took a great quantity of bronze.

When Tou king of Hamath heard that David had
defeated the entire army of Hadadezer, he sent his son
Joram to King David to greet him and congratulate him
on his victory in battle over Hadadezer, who had been at
war with Tou. Joram brought with him articles of silver, of
gold and of bronze. King David dedicated these articles
to the LORD, *as he had done with the silver and gold from*
all the nations he had subdued: Edom and Moab, the
Ammonites and the Philistines, and Amalek.

He also dedicated the plunder taken from Hadadezer
son of Rehob, king of Zobah. And David became
famous after he returned from striking down eighteen
thousand Edomites in the Valley of Salt. He put garrisons
throughout Edom, and all the Edomites became subject to
David. The LORD *gave David victory wherever he went.* "

(2 Samuel 8:1-14)

These conquests are confirmed in the book of Kings, which also describes the extent of territories ruled over by Solomon, David's son, stretching all the way down to the border of Egypt:

> *"The people of Judah and Israel were as numerous as the sand on the seashore; they ate, they drank and they were happy. And Solomon ruled over all the kingdoms from the Euphrates River to the land of the Philistines, as far as the border of Egypt. These countries brought tribute and were Solomon's subjects all his life.*
>
> *Solomon's daily provisions were thirty cors of the finest flour and sixty cors of meal, ten head of stall-fed cattle, twenty of pasture-fed cattle and a hundred sheep and goats, as well as deer, gazelles, roebucks and choice fowl. For he ruled over all the kingdoms west of the Euphrates River, from Tiphsah* (on the south bank of the Euphrates, in the area running through northern Syria, north east of Damascus) *to Gaza, and had peace on all sides. During Solomon's lifetime Judah and Israel, from Dan to Beersheba, lived in safety, everyone under their own vine and fig tree."*

(1 Kings 4:20-25)

So all the territory promised to Abraham eventually came under Israel's dominion and consisted of present day Lebanon and Syria south of the Euphrates, plus territories to the east the River Jordan and the Dead Sea. Today, this is the western part of Jordan in the region surrounding Amman, the capital, and the area south towards the northern Negev.

God gave Solomon great wisdom and as there was no blood on his hands from conquering all the above mentioned kingdoms, he was allowed to build the Temple in Jerusalem. He later succumbed to the charms of numerous women who led him to worship their gods. This great sin caused God to divide the kingdom in two, Israel to the north and Judah in the south, with the eventual exile of both. By New Testament times, the original borders had become greatly reduced but were still larger than those which are being disputed today.

Romans 13:1-7 clearly tells us that God continues to work through national governments to bring law and order within a country, verse 4, as well as through their armies to defend borders against invasion etc. Jesus taught that *"if you live by the sword you will die by the sword"*, *Matt. 26:52*, which not only applies to individuals but to nations as well. For instance, God used the Israelite nation to bring a righteous judgment on the Canaanites and Hittites etc. who were using the knife to sacrifice their own children! Through this He gave the Israelites their land. God also justly dismantled the Turkish Empire because they fought alongside the Germans in World War I and slaughtered around one million Armenian Christians. Through this action He freed Israel from Turkish Muslim domination. We also saw God using Britain and her Allies to stop Hitler in World War II, which uprooted the Jews from Europe. He will continue to use this application of justice to restore all the territories promised to Abraham. God will deal with any nation that acts in a consistently evil manner and is unwilling to change. If their land belongs to the Jews by promise, He will use the situation to return it to Israel.

So Joshua and King David conquered all the land covenanted to them but foolishly they did not carry out God's judgment of putting all to the sword. They compromised and are still paying the price for this disobedience.

Significantly, there is a correlation between physical Israel and spiritual Israel, the Church. As the Jews went through exile in other nations because of disobedience, losing nearly all their spiritual insight, so the Church went through the Dark Ages where understanding of the new birth etc. was lost. But praise God, over the centuries the Reformation has seen a steady restoration of New Testament truths that still continue to this day. It will go on until together we reach full maturity and possesses the whole spiritual Promised Land in Christ. Like Israel today, the Church is only living in part of "her inheritance" and has many opposing views on various subjects. But Jesus is building His Church and will bring us to the unity of the faith, which means we will receive our doctrine from the Holy Spirit rather than from our clever ideas. God is raising up the five-fold ministry to achieve this and the apostle Paul put it this way:

"Christ himself gave the apostles, the prophets, the evangelists, the pastors and teachers, to equip his people for works of service, so that the body of Christ may be built up until we all reach unity in the faith and in the knowledge of the Son of God and become mature, attaining to the whole measure of the fullness of Christ."

(Ephesians 4:11-13)

This maturity is what Jesus was referring to when He said:

"Very truly I tell you, all who have faith in me will do the works I have been doing, and they will do even greater things than these, because I am going to the Father."

(John 14:12)

We are going to see God restoring all the land to the Jews, with the whole Jewish nation becoming born again and on fire for Jesus Christ!

12 *Europe and Islam*

To understand what is developing in Europe we need to take a look at what the scriptures say about today's situation. Several visions in Daniel and Revelation provide great clarity as to what is happening. In Rev. 17:3-11 we see a seven headed beast ridden by the Mother of Prostitutes:

> *"³Then the angel carried me away in the Spirit into a wilderness. There I saw a woman sitting on a scarlet beast that was covered with blasphemous names and had seven heads and ten horns. ⁴The woman was dressed in purple and scarlet, and was glittering with gold, precious stones and pearls. She held a golden cup in her hand, filled with abominable things and the filth of her adulteries. ⁵The name written on her forehead was a mystery:*

> BABYLON THE GREAT
> THE MOTHER OF PROSTITUTES AND OF
> THE ABOMINATIONS OF THE EARTH

> *⁶I saw that the woman was drunk with the blood of God's holy people, the blood of those who bore testimony to*

*Jesus. When I saw her, I was greatly astonished. ⁷Then
the angel said to me: "Why are you astonished? I will
explain to you the mystery of the woman and of the beast
she rides, which has the seven heads and ten horns. ⁸The
beast, which you saw, once was, now is not, and yet will
come up out of the Abyss and go to its destruction. The
inhabitants of the earth whose names have not been
written in the book of life from the creation of the world
will be astonished when they see the beast, because it once
was, now is not, and yet will come. ⁹This calls for a mind
with wisdom. The seven heads are seven hills on which the
woman sits. ¹⁰They are also seven kings* (kingdoms). *Five
have fallen, one is, the other has not yet come; but when
he does come, he must remain for only a little while. ¹¹The
beast who once was, and now is not, is an eighth king. He
belongs to the seven and is going to his destruction."*

(Revelation 17:3-11)

The Mother of Prostitutes symbolizes Satan and the religious
systems he and his fellow demons have birthed and developed
to rob God of His rightful worship. The seven headed beast
also refers to Satan, but here it represents the political powers
he has manipulated which have ruled over the Jewish nation.
Just as the person who rides a horse is in charge of directing
it, so the priests and their beliefs control and direct the politics
of these empires. There is a full explanation of all this in
Almost Midnight.

To summarize the above quote, God gives two interpretations
of the seven heads. In the first one, verse 9, the apostle John
clearly understood that the seven hills were those on which
Rome was built. Here, the woman symbolized the priests

and gods of Rome who were later replaced by the religion that eventually took control, namely Roman Catholicism headed up by the Popes. Both religious groups persecuted true born again Christians. In the second interpretation of the seven heads, they each represent an empire. The key to understanding this second meaning is that all the empires dealt with in the Bible are only those who have ruled over the Jews. There are many such as India, China and the U.S.A. etc but they are never included because the Bible is a book that only deals with the Jews and those individual believers who become sons of Abraham through faith in Christ. The first five heads of verse 10 are therefore the Egyptians, Assyrians, Babylonians, Persians and Greeks. The Romans were the sixth head, the *"one is"*, as they ruled the Jews at the time of John's writing. He was imprisoned in a Roman penal colony on the Isle of Patmos for preaching the gospel.

But what is the seventh head of verse 10, which has not yet come and will remain for only a little while? The vision of the enormous statue given by God to the Babylonian king, Nebuchadnezzar, Dan. 2, identifies it. The statue represents the last four empires that have ruled over Israel – the head of gold was the Babylonians, the two arms and chest of silver were the Persians and Medes, the belly and two thighs of bronze symbolize the Greeks whose empire was later divided to the north and south of Israel. The two legs of iron represent the Roman Empire which separated into east and west for ease of governance. The feet were partly iron and partly baked clay, which do not mix. It is very important to see that the iron continues right down through the feet to all 10 toes – the 10 end-time kingdoms. This shows us that although the western part of the Roman Empire met its demise in 476 AD, with a similar collapse happening later in the east, the empire continues in some form until the end of this age, albeit diminished in power. The seventh head therefore represents a revival of the Roman Empire but with reduced strength and disharmony in it due to the clay.

Rev. 17:11, quoted above, tells us that an eighth head will emerge from the beast, which is the Antichrist, but it says he is destined for destruction. Jesus lived on earth in the time of the two legs when the empire was at its full strength. There was no clay present then. His return is represented by the Rock that smashes the feet and toes, causing the whole statue to disintegrate. This means that the 10 end-time kingdoms will be present at the time of the glorious appearance of Jesus when He will destroy the accumulation of all the false religions and rebellious ways of man that have occurred throughout the age, and liberate Israel from the tyranny.

Daniel is given a further vision of these same four last empires that have ruled over the Jews but this time they are described as different beasts. The last beast, representing the Roman Empire, has 10 horns which is another way of describing the 10 end-time kingdoms, Dan. 7:1-8. Again, this empire is shown continuing until the end of this age and the triumphant return of Jesus, Dan. 7:15-27. Three of the 10 horns are uprooted by a little horn (the Antichrist), which speaks against the Most High, Dan. 7:25, i.e. three of the 10 end-time kingdoms are overturned by the Antichrist as they cease to support him at some stage. Daniel's visions in chapters 2 and 7 are saying that the 10 end-time nations and the Antichrist will emerge from the revived Roman Empire, and not from anywhere else. The spirits that governed it in John's day are actively involved in developing this seventh head in the supposed glory of the original Roman Empire, ruled over spiritually by Roman Catholicism.

I believe the European Union is this seventh power and it is no coincidence that it was established by the Treaty of Rome at the initial E.E.C. stage. The flag also has great significance as the stars on it do not represent the number of nations in the union, which currently stands at 27. The motif on the flag is based on a stained glass window in the Roman Catholic Cathedral at Strasburg, picturing the Virgin Mary. She is seen there with twelve golden stars around her head, all on a blue background, from which the flag design is taken. The stars symbolize the 12 tribes of Israel as described in Rev.12:1-6. Here, the woman is clothed with the sun, and the moon is under her feet. As previously explained in chapter 8, the typology is deliberately chosen by the Lord to link the reader to the vision He gave Joseph in Egypt regarding his family, Gen. 37:9-10. Mistakenly, Catholicism believes the woman in Revelation 12 refers solely to Mary. Although Mary is intimately involved, having given birth to Jesus, the vision actually refers to the whole nation of Israel, and her offspring are Gentile believers in Christ. We know it cannot just be symbolizing Mary as the "woman" continues to feature at the end of chapter 12 when the End-time years are described. All this should come as no surprise as Roman Catholics, such as Jean Monnet, were architects of the vision to unite Europe by restoring the Holy Roman Empire in modern clothes. Thankfully, Rev. 17:10 says that when this seventh empire comes to power it will only last a short time.

As pointed out, each material mentioned in the Daniel 2 statue symbolizes a different power that has dominated Israel, and the baked clay introduced into the iron in the feet and toes, is no exception. Some have speculated that the clay refers to democracy which has developed in Europe, but this has actually brought flexibility rather than the brittleness that baked clay pictures. Since the full Roman Empire, the time of pure iron, the only major power that has dominated Israel for any length of time is Islam. This began in 638 AD when Muslim Arabs invaded Jerusalem. Islam is not just a religion but a political power which desires to replace and rule over all other systems. The scripture says that just as baked clay cannot mix with iron, so this power cannot mix with the traditions of Europe, and I believe this describes Islam perfectly. Although we have seen it infiltrate into European countries and elsewhere, Islam is incapable of integrating. It believes itself to be superior to all other political and religious beliefs and must introduce Sharia law for people to be acceptable before Allah. The Jihad (a Holy War for Allah) of the Ottoman Empire in 1683 was successfully stopped at Vienna by the valiant Polish army but today's tactics of immigration are proving more effective for their cause.

The world has never endorsed full biblical Christianity such as the new birth, but even its fundamental morals are now openly challenged and ridiculed. I believe that as the global faith alliance gathers strength, the mutually exclusive doctrines within each religion will be voluntarily removed and militancy between faiths will be outlawed. For instance, true Islam teaches that it is the duty of Muslims to kill anyone who converts from Islam, Sura 4:89, as well as being mandatory for all Muslims to join Jihad against infidels of other faiths who reject Islam, Sura 9:29. But contrary to this, liberal Islam today is altering the meaning of Jihad from Muhammad's teaching to now mean the fight against injustice rather than against those who reject Islam. This is to comply with the growing movement throughout the world to bring an alliance of world religions. Every person will be free to worship or not as he wishes, but any faith which says that its particular set of beliefs is the only way to God will not be tolerated. Militant Islam and born again Christianity etc. therefore will be increasingly outlawed.

It must be said that there are many genuine born again believers in the Catholic Church despite the gross unbiblical errors that it teaches and there are many upright and good citizens in Islam. It is not the people who are the problem but the doctrines of these two faiths.

In September 2011, President Abbas of the West Bank Fatah Party presented the Palestinians' request for full statehood to the U.N. which, if accepted, would have given them a seat in the General Assembly. The U.S.A. made it very clear that they would veto this unilateral move as there must be mutual agreement with Israel to have any hope of peace between the two peoples. The two parties have been given a further 12 months to reach a compromise agreement. This, together with the financial crisis in Europe where there is a lack of clear, wise and strong leadership, is setting the scene for the end-time Antichrist to enter the world's stage and solve its problems.

13 *The Last Seven Years*

I would like to briefly recap and enlarge on what has already been said so we are clear in our minds as regards the duration of the end years, as this will be very important for those of us who will go through them. I explained in chapter 5 that the last seven years of this age complete the 490 year decree over the Jews and Jerusalem, Dan. 9:24-27. In chapter 8 we saw that each of these last seven years is made up of 360 days. The first 483 years ended with the crucifixion in 33 AD and when we calculated these years in terms of 360 days each, they reduced down to 476 solar years bringing secular history into a perfect fit with the Bible. There is an approximate 2,000 year time gap from the cross to the start of the last seven years. Again I deal with these points in more detail in *Almost Midnight*.

The events during this last week of years are described in Revelation chapters 6 to 19. Very significantly, there is more Jewish phraseology here than chapters 2-3 as they are concluding the last seven years of God's 490 year decree concerning the Jewish nation. Chapters 4 and 5 describe the throne room in heaven with 24 elders. Examples of Jewishness from chapters 6 onwards include coloured horses riding out similar to Zechariah's vision, Zech. 1:7-11; 144,000 very zealous Jews becoming part of the Church then being sealed and accepting celibacy like the apostle Paul; John being commanded to eat a scroll as Ezekiel did; temple worship; terrifying beasts as in Daniel; the two witnesses prophesying in Jerusalem; the false prophet − presumably mimicking Elijah; plagues similar to those in Moses time; Babylon being judged and so on.

God described Satan as the morning star. Tragically, pride overcame him and he was no longer content with being the brightest and highest angel. He wanted to be like God and be worshipped. After being cast out of heaven, along with one third of the angels who had joined in the rebellion, he became jealous of Adam and Eve because they had taken first place in God's heart on the newly formed earth. His plan to deal with the situation was to entice the couple to sin, bringing them out of relationship with God. Not only was he envious of them being made in God's image, Gen. 1:26, he was also after their submission and adoration. Satan and his fellow rebels have been able to lead mankind into all manner of false religions where they are deified. Indeed, Paul describes Satan as the "god of this world", 2 Cor. 4:4.

"How you have fallen from heaven, morning star, son of the dawn! You have been cast down to the earth, you who once laid low the nations! You said in your heart, "I will ascend to heaven; I will raise my throne above the stars (angels) *of God; I will sit enthroned on the mount of assembly, on the utmost heights of the sacred mountain. I will ascend above the tops of the clouds; I will make*

myself like the Most High." *[15]But you are brought down to the realm of the dead, to the depths of the pit.*"

(Isaiah 14:12-15)

This revelation was given in the middle of a prophecy against Babylon, Is. 14:4-23. God was not only speaking against the King of Babylon but also to the spirit motivating him, namely Satan, whose desire to be worshipped like God remains unabated. Central to his objective is to place his man, the Antichrist, on the throne in Jerusalem. Satan knows that this city is where Jesus will reign over all the earth as King of kings, so he is hellbent on usurping the throne for the Antichrist. Unlike Jesus, who refused Satan's offer of all the earthly kingdoms in exchange for worshipping him, Luke 4:5-8, this Man of Sin will delight in the thought of world power and adulation by the masses. However, God has long decreed his downfall in verse 15 above.

The Devil intends to raise the Antichrist to international prominence through a combination of increased political power and an alliance of world religions. He will establish a One World Government arising out of the revived Roman Empire. Satan's ploy to preach an "all roads lead to God" theology will be highly acceptable to the vast majority as well, as it promises some form of hope and peace to a world faced with escalating turmoil in the nations. It will lead up to the last seven years.

We are told that all people will want to follow and worship both the Antichrist and his god because of a miraculous healing and his military power:

"³One of the heads of the beast (the eighth) **seemed**
to have had a fatal wound, but the fatal wound had
been healed. The whole world was filled with wonder
and followed the beast. ⁴People worshiped the dragon
because he had given authority to the beast, and they also
worshiped the beast and asked, "Who is like the beast?
Who can make war against it?"

(Revelation 13:3-4)

It looks like this seemingly fatal wound and dramatic recovery,
verse 3, will mimic the death and resurrection of Jesus. The
Antichrist may even appear to be dead for three days before
he "comes back to life". Whatever happens, it must be very
spectacular for the whole world to be filled with wonder and
follow him. Through this supposed supernatural recovery,
the Antichrist will himself be encouraged to believe he is the
Messiah. He will not understand about dying for the sins of
mankind but as the world is oblivious to that need, it will not
be a problem.

Through all these spectacular events he will be fully
supported by the False Prophet and both will rise to world
leadership. The latter is able to perform miraculous signs, as
Satan gives him power e.g. causing fire to come down from
the sky, Rev.13:11-14, similar to when Elijah destroyed the
prophets of Baal, 1 Kings 18:36-39. God has promised that
the true Elijah will come again before the great and terrible
day of the Lord and that true believers will recognise him,
Malachi 4:5. I believe he will be one of the two witnesses
who prophesy in Jerusalem for 1,260 days.

Satan knows he has to fool the Jewish religious community
into believing the Antichrist is the Messiah in order to

convince the Jews to rebuild the Temple. At the moment he is using militant Islam to change the political and spiritual landscape in the Middle East, to unseat the Jewish hold on Jerusalem and open it up for all religions. But I believe this violent fundamentalism will be outlawed at some point in favour of a non violent version of Islam. Encouraging all peaceful religions, including Mosaic Judaism, will also allow the Antichrist to lead the Jews back into temple sacrifice.

The Jews have already made ready the Levitical regalia and geneticians are even now working on producing a red heifer for purification according to the law, Num. 19:2. The religious Jews are aware that the Psalmist said, *"unless the Lord builds the house they labour in vain"*, Ps. 127:1 and so they will not build the Temple until the Messiah comes and authorises it. Their animal sacrifices, according to the Mosaic law, can then commence. This will see Daniel's prophecy come to pass, *"He* (the Antichrist) *will confirm a* (the) *covenant with many for one seven"*, *Dan. 9:27.* All this may well be part of a peace treaty between the Israelis and Palestinians, but only the act of Temple sacrifice will start the clock ticking on the last seven years. Leading up to, and during the first three and a half years, an increasing number of Jews will come to faith in Christ. But the majority will still hold out against God, even though they are earnestly going through the Old Covenant Temple rituals, because it is without true faith in God.

Daniel 9:27 informs us that the Antichrist will reinstate sacrifice for the Jews at the beginning of the seven years as part of the encouragement of all world religions to practise their own traditions and work together. We are already seeing this happening today. The Pope has been organising joint prayer meetings in Assisi with the Dalai Lama, Hindus,

Buddhists, liberal Christians and liberal Muslims etc. and this is just the tip of the iceberg.

The Muslims are waiting for their Mahdi, the final Caliph, to unite Islam and reign for seven years from Jerusalem, imposing Sharia law which they believe will bring peace to the earth. The spirits of Islam have taken this last seven year revelation from the Bible and modified it to further deceive their followers. The Freemasons are the only group who could feasibly co-operate with the Jews and construct a Temple. David Rockefeller, a 33 Degree Mason and not a Jew, has already drawn up plans for one to be built on the Temple plinth to the northern side of the Dome of the Rock. This would stand facing the Golden Gate to the east. The New Age movement also sees Jerusalem as a main gateway to the supernatural realm, and there are other religious groups who would like to worship there as well.

Paul describes the Antichrist as the "lawless one", as quoted below, because he is totally opposed to all the laws of God in the Bible. His initial encouragement for Jews to observe the law will just be a deception. I believe he is currently in the world right now and Satan is positioning him for his rise to prominence. But he will be constrained by the Holy Spirit from implementing the final part of his evil plan to take absolute control until the first seal is broken. The Father will then instruct the Spirit to step aside to allow him to do so:

> *"For the secret power of lawlessness is already at work; but the one who now holds it back* (the Holy Spirit) *will continue to do so till He is taken out of the way. **And then the lawless one will be revealed**, whom the Lord Jesus will overthrow with the breath of his mouth and destroy by the*

splendor of his coming. The coming of the lawless one will
be in accordance with how Satan works. He will use all
sorts of displays of power through signs and wonders that
serve the lie, and all the ways that wickedness deceives
those who are perishing. They perish because they refused
to love the truth and so be saved. For this reason God
sends them a powerful delusion so that they will believe
the lie and so that all will be condemned who have not
believed the truth but have delighted in wickedness."

(2 Thessalonians 2:7-12)

This will be similar to the situation with Judas at the Last
Supper. Satan was unable to touch Jesus, but there came a
time when Jesus gave permission to Judas to carry out the
evil deed he had decided upon in his heart, and Satan then
entered him, John 13:18-30. Jesus was never dictated to by
the situation because He followed the Holy Spirit's leading
and likewise the Spirit will guide us right through to the end,
if we listen to Him.

The first white horse of the apocalypse refers to the end-
time Antichrist riding out with a bow and crown to conquer
the nations, declaring he is the Messiah who must be obeyed
and that his rightful place is on the throne in Jerusalem
from where he will rule the world. Jesus never came to
conquer men but to set people free. Amazingly, we see that
it is Jesus who gives the Antichrist his power just as God
gave Nebuchadnezzar authority over the nations in his day,
Dan. 2:37-38.

"I watched as the Lamb opened the first of the seven seals.
Then I heard one of the four living creatures say in a voice

like thunder, "Come!" I looked, and there before me was
a white horse! Its rider held a bow, and he was given a
crown, and he rode out as a conqueror bent on conquest. "

(Revelation 6:1-2, 2 Thess. 2:1-3)

It is the breaking of this seal which starts the Day of the Lord,
as it allows the Antichrist to move from just deceiving the world
to taking dictatorial power over the earth (2 Thess. 2:1-3).
Freedom for peaceful religions, including Judaism, will be
replaced by compulsory worship of the Antichrist and his Higher
Power (Satan). This second phase will quickly see temple
sacrifice abolished and so the next part of Daniel's prophecy
will then be fulfilled, *"In the middle of the seven* (the last seven
years) *he will put an end to sacrifice and offering"*, Dan. 9:27.
The exact point at which the seal is broken is not given but
it will be towards the end of the first three and a half years.
The Antichrist's reign of terror will last 42 judgment months
(1,260 days), starting from the abolition of Temple sacrifice:

"The beast was given a mouth to utter proud words and
blasphemies and to exercise its authority for forty-two
months (three and a half judgment years). *It opened its*
mouth to blaspheme God, and to slander his name and his
dwelling place and those who live in heaven. It was given
power to wage war against God's holy people and to
conquer them. And it was given authority over every tribe,
people, language and nation. All inhabitants of the earth
will worship the beast—all whose names have not been
written in the Lamb's book of life, the Lamb who was slain
from the creation of the world. "

(Revelation 13:5-8)

Breaking the next three seals releases the red, black and pale horses of end-time wars, famines and deaths respectively. Interestingly, the colour of the fourth horse in the original Greek text, Rev. 6:8, is *"chloros"*. We derive our word chlorine, chlorophyll etc. from this word. Elsewhere in the New Testament it is translated as a vegetational green, not just an unspecified pale colour. Both Mark 3:39 and Rev. 8:7 use it to describe green grass and John also speaks of green plants, bushes and trees, Rev. 9:4. So the fourth horse is actually a mid green. My question is, has this anything to do with the green colour of Islam, which is certainly a religion causing much mayhem and death throughout the world, otherwise described as baked clay in the feet of the great statue vision in Daniel 2?

As explained, under Satan's instructions the Antichrist will enthrone himself in the Temple as God and absolute ruler over the earth. Paul warns us of this:

"He (the Antichrist) *will oppose and will exalt himself*
over everything that is called God or is worshipped,
so that he sets himself up in God's temple, proclaiming
himself to be God."

(2 Thessalonians 2:4)

Any peace treaty that may arise between Israel and the Palestinians before or in conjunction with reinstatement of Temple sacrifice will likely be planned to last for far more than seven years, but the Bible makes it clear for those who listen to God, that the Antichrist will definitely stop the offerings after three and a half years, and probably any treaty as well, in favour of compulsory worship of himself and his god. This rejection of Judaism will greatly help those Jews who haven't already converted to Christianity to see through his gigantic deception and cause a genuine seeking of God who will then be able to reveal Christ to them. Paul prophesied that those Jews who survive the Tribulation will be saved, Rom. 11:26.

The Antichrist is supported in his diabolical activities by the 10 end-time nations, Rev. 17:12-18, and together they will destroy every religious practice. Amazingly, we see here that God will use the Antichrist to judge all the different faiths of this world! Unfortunately, he will not differentiate between false faiths and the true faith of Christianity, Rev. 13:15-18.

"The ten horns (the 10 end-time nations evolving from the E.U.) *you saw are ten kings who have not yet received a kingdom, but who **for one hour** will receive authority as kings along with the beast* (the Antichrist). *They have one purpose and will give their power and authority to the beast. They will wage war against the Lamb, but the Lamb will triumph over them because he is Lord of lords and King of kings—and with him will be his called, chosen and faithful followers.*

Then the angel said to me, the waters you saw, where the prostitute (the false religions that have dominated the nations) *sits, are peoples, multitudes, nations and languages. The beast and the ten horns you saw will hate the prostitute. They will bring her to ruin and leave her naked; they will eat her flesh and burn her with fire. For God has put it into their hearts to accomplish his purpose by agreeing to hand over to the beast their royal authority, until God's words are fulfilled. **The woman you saw is the great city that rules over the kings of the earth.**"*

(Revelation 17:12-18)

"The woman who rides the beast", *Rev. 17:3-11,* represents the religious authorities who rule the political powers, and is described by God here as a city. The above verses also confirm that the 10 end-time kingdoms and the Antichrist will only last a short time, *"for one hour"*.

Paul wrote that it is *"Jesus, who rescues us from the coming wrath"*, *1 Thess.1:10.* As I have shown in chapter 9 this does not mean He takes the Church out of the world before the Tribulation commences. He saves us within it! The Church will be saved from God's wrath just like the Jews were saved from His judgments on Pharaoh (a type of the end-time Antichrist) before the Jews came out of Egypt. This is also similar to God saving Noah in the Ark from the judgment water. The Ark represents Christ, of course, and the same amount of rain (judgment) fell on Noah as it did on those outside, but he and his family were kept "dry as a bone" in it. So the Church will be kept secure in Christ from all the boils etc. that God pours out on those resisting Him during this horrendous time. The Bible says not one plague from God will touch a Christian during the Tribulation providing he walks closely with the Lord: Rev. 18:4.

> *"Then I heard another voice from heaven say: 'Come out of her, my people, so that you will not share in her sins, so that you will not receive any of her plagues'"*
>
> (Revelation 18:4)

However, believers will be persecuted by those who reject Jesus and many will be killed for their testimony of Him, just as the Jews were treated as slaves by the Egyptians. Likewise, the people rejected Noah's message to repent and scoffed at him for building a large boat in the middle of the desert. Jesus said

"As it was in the days of Noah, so it will be at the coming of the Son of Man... two men will be working in the field: one will be taken and the other left", Matt. 24:37-40. The last part of this is speaking of the rapture that happens at the return of Jesus.

Proudly and very foolishly, the Antichrist believes he can fight Jesus and win but as we know, the Bible says pride goes before a fall:

> *"Then I saw the beast and the kings of the earth and their armies gathered together to make war against the rider* (Jesus) *on the horse and his army. But the beast was captured, and with him the false prophet who had performed the signs on his behalf. With these signs he had deluded those who had received the mark of the beast and worshiped his image. The two of them were thrown alive into the fiery lake of burning sulphur. The rest were killed with the sword coming out of the mouth of the rider on the horse, and all the birds gorged themselves on their flesh."*
>
> (Revelation 19:19-21)

The purpose of all the wrath and turmoil poured out by God is to show people His anger at their rejection of Jesus' sacrifice, and to undermine their self sufficiency so as many as possible will turn to Jesus for salvation. All the way through the book of Revelation after the various judgments are brought, we see the comment *"and still they did not repent"*. God's heart is that all men should be saved. Another major objective is that He might fulfil His promise to Abraham to bring the Jewish nation to repentance and faith in their Messiah before the end of this age. This will mean world events increasingly centering on Jerusalem. It may well become an international city as envisaged by the UN in 1947 but never implemented to date. As mentioned, all the major religions want to worship there!

At the very end of the seven years, Jesus will return in a display of awesome power never before witnessed on earth. He will destroy all rebellion and cast both the Antichrist and the False Prophet into the Lake of Fire, Rev. 19:20. These are the only two who do not come before the Judgment Throne at the end. Jesus will slay all who have the *"Mark of the Beast", Rev. 13:18*, who have not repented, and they will be held captive in Hell until Judgment Day at the end of the 1,000 year millennial reign of Christ, along with those who have rejected God's Word down through the ages.

Not only will we see a dramatic change in Israel but we are told of seismic events to the north and south of her, in both Egypt and Syria. Biblically, this includes Egypt, Syria and their present day neighbours.

> *"In that day there will be an altar to the LORD* (the cross, since Jesus) *in the heart of Egypt, and a monument to the LORD at its border. It will be a sign and witness to the LORD Almighty in the land of Egypt. When they cry out to the LORD because of their oppressors, he will send them a saviour and defender, and he will rescue them. So the LORD will make himself known to the Egyptians, and in that day they will acknowledge the LORD. They will worship with sacrifices and grain offerings; they will make vows to the LORD and keep them. The LORD will strike Egypt with a plague; he will strike them and heal them. They will turn to the LORD, and he will respond to their pleas and heal them* (they will have a difficult road like the Jews, as their hearts have also been hard towards God).

In that day there will be a highway from Egypt to Assyria.
The Assyrians will go to Egypt and the Egyptians to
Assyria. The Egyptians and Assyrians will worship
together (in Christ). *In that day Israel will be the third,*
along with Egypt and Assyria, a blessing on the earth.
The LORD Almighty will bless them, saying, "Blessed be
Egypt my people, Assyria my handiwork, and Israel my
inheritance (also in Christ). *"*

(Isaiah 19:19-25)

It seems that these verses refer to events before Jesus returns,
but Zechariah warns that plagues are still being inflicted on
people who do not go up to Jerusalem to worship Jesus during
the Millennium:

"Then the survivors from all the nations that have
attacked Jerusalem will go up year after year to worship
the King, the Lord Almighty, and to celebrate the Festival
of Tabernacles. If any of the peoples of the earth do not
go up to Jerusalem to worship the King (Jesus), *the Lord*
Almighty, they will have no rain. If the Egyptian people do
not go up and take part, they will have no rain. The Lord
will bring on them the plague he inflicts on the nations
that do not go up. "

(Zechariah 14:16-18)

From this scripture it looks like the Millennium is not the
perfect utopian paradise that some imagine but it will be a
time of unprecedented peace because Jesus is reigning there
and Satan is locked up.

14 *"No One Knows About that Day or Hour... but only the Father"*

Because of all these major upheavals in the earth, God has graciously given us some additional timings regarding the very end of the Tribulation which are vital for us to look at and understand. Within the relevant scriptures there is another confirmation that Jerusalem is seen as holy, even after the Jews rejected and crucified their Messiah in 33 AD. Matthew writes, *"After Jesus' resurrection they went into the holy city"*, *Matt. 27:53*. This is yet further proof that God still considers the city set aside for Himself. John confirmed this holy status but also predicted the awful prospect that Gentiles would again dominate Jerusalem at the end of this age, even though the Jews had regained sovereignty of their city in 1967. He wrote *"they* (the Gentiles) *will trample the holy city for 42 months"*, *Rev. 11:2*. After Temple sacrifice is abolished the Antichrist will reign in Jerusalem during these three and a half judgment years. This imposition is due to the Jews' continued stubbornness against accepting Jesus as their

Messiah, which ensures further punishment according to the Mosaic law:

> *"It will be for a time, times and half a time. When the power of the holy people has been finally broken, all these things will be completed."*
>
> (Daniel 12:7)

This period will see the two witnesses start preaching in the city that all must repent and trust in the Lordship of Jesus Christ. One of them will definitely be Elijah, Malachi 4:5, but the other may well be Moses who will explain clearly how the law was designed to lead the Jews to their Messiah, Jesus:

> *"And I will give power to my two witnesses, and they will prophesy for 1,260 days* (42 months or 3.5 judgment years)...*Now when they have finished their testimony, the beast* (Satan) *that comes up from the Abyss will attack them, and overpower and kill them. Their bodies will lie in the public square of the great city* (Jerusalem), *which is figuratively called Sodom and Egypt, where also their Lord was crucified. For three and a half days many from every people, tribe, language and nation will gaze on their bodies and refuse them burial. The inhabitants of the earth will gloat over them and will celebrate by sending each other gifts, because these two prophets had tormented those who live on the earth. But after the three and a half days the breath of life from God entered them, and they stood on their feet, and terror struck those who saw them."*
>
> (Revelation. 11:3-12)

The Antichrist cannot touch them for those 1,260 days until their time of preaching is completed. God then allows them to be slain and their bodies are left out in the street for all to see. The whole world will rejoice at their deaths. However, three and a half days later, God will raise them from the dead, bringing terror to the hearts of those who rejected their message and celebrated their murder. He will take the two witnesses up to heaven in the sight of all.

It is Daniel who provides further details of extreme importance on the timing of events immediately after their astonishing recovery and ascension.

"From the time that the daily (Temple) *sacrifice is abolished and the abomination that causes desolation is set up, there will be 1,290 days.*

Blessed is the one who waits for and reaches the end **of the 1,335 days.** "

(Daniel 12:11-12)

The abolition of Temple sacrifice half way through the last seven years is a pivotal event from which these two above timings follow. There are 1,260 days from its inception up to its abolition. Daniel informs us that 1,290 days after the sacrifice is stopped, the False Prophet sets up an image of the Antichrist that people will be forced to worship, Rev. 13:15-17. This would be 30 days after the two witnesses are killed (1,260 + 30 = 1,290). Secondly, there will be 1,335 days from the abolition to the glorious and spectacular return of Jesus which brings this age to a close. Mercifully, the Lord is saying that the idol in the Temple will only be tolerated by God for a maximum of 45 days (1,290 + 45 = 1,335), because at Jesus' return He destroys the image and casts the Antichrist and the False Prophet into the lake of fire. It is a great relief to know that there will only be these relatively few days in which those who refuse to bow down and worship the effigy are executed, and those who reject the 666 mark are excluded from the world's financial system.

Jesus would have been very aware of this 1,335 day period when He explained the end-time events to the Jews. He said His return would be preceded by a period of unequalled distress, *"If those days had not been cut short, no one would survive, but for the sake of the elect those days will be shortened"*, *Matt. 24:22*. He recognized that there was a predetermined time to His return which would be brought forward for the sake of the elect, those that had put their faith in Him. He went on to say that the Father alone would decide by how many days this would be - *"no one knows about that day or hour...but only the Father"*, *Matt. 24:36*.

Regarding the "mark of the beast", the book of Revelation is written in Greek and each letter has a numerical value in that language. For instance, the value of Iesous, Jesus' name in Greek, is 888. Eight in the Bible stands for new and abundant life. Six is the number of man – Adam was formed on the sixth day etc. 666 is the epitome of man in rebellion to God i.e. death. The biblical meaning of death is spiritual separation from God. I therefore believe the Antichrist's name will add up to this number. Be careful, however, as there will be many things that total 666 and just be coincidental. But when all the other points mentioned in the Bible are exhibited by one man and his name comes to this figure, it will confirm who the man of sin is:

"Because of the signs it (the False Prophet, which is the second beast) *was given power to perform on behalf of the first beast* (the Antichrist), *it deceived the inhabitants of the earth. It ordered them to set up an image in honor of the beast who was wounded by the sword and yet lived. The second beast was given power to give breath to the image of the first beast, so that the image could speak and cause all who refused to worship the image to be killed. It also forced all people, great and small, rich and poor, free and slave, to receive a mark on their right hands or on their foreheads, so that they could not buy or sell unless they had the mark, which is the name of the beast or the number of its name. This calls for wisdom. Let the person who has insight calculate the number of the beast, for it is the number of a man. That number is 666."*

(Revelation 13:14-18)

We know it is within this maximum period of 45 days that the last seven bowls (plagues) of God's wrath are poured out because the first plague only falls on those who have the 666 mark:

*"I saw in heaven another great and marvelous sign: seven angels with the **seven** last **plagues —last, because with them God's wrath is completed.**"*

(Revelation 15:1)

"The first angel went and poured out his bowl on the land, and ugly, festering sores broke out on the people who had the mark of the beast and worshiped its image."

(Revelation 16:2)

The whole world will be subjected to these last devastating judgments, which will also affect the Antichrist's seat of power in Jerusalem. But as we have shown, God says Christians will not be touched directly by them as long as they are not following the world's ways.

> *"The fourth angel poured out his bowl on the sun, and the sun was allowed to scorch people with fire. They were seared by the intense heat and they cursed the name of God, who had control over these plagues, but they refused to repent and glorify him. The fifth angel poured out his bowl on the throne of the beast, and its kingdom was plunged into darkness. People gnawed their tongues in agony and cursed the God of heaven because of their pains and their sores, but they refused to repent of what they had done."*
>
> (Revelation 16:10-11)

This scripture says that the people did not repent even though they knew God was the source of their torment. One can also conclude from this that a person can still repent and be saved even if they have gladly complied with the Antichrist and received his mark. But it must be a genuine turning to God. Those who have the 666 mark and are not repentant continue to endure the full force of the bowls and will be slain by Jesus at His return, Rev. 19:19-21.

The 490 judgment years spoken of in the decree over the Jews and Jerusalem are complete after the second 1,260 days. The additional 75 days (1,260+30+45) only concern the Antichrist and his followers, when the statue of the Antichrist is set up and the last of God's judgments are poured out on them through the seven bowls. The latter part of Dan. 9:27 explains the decree God made regarding the Antichrist: *"And at the temple he* (the Antichrist) *will set up an abomination* (the image of the Antichrist) *that causes desolation, until the end that is decreed is poured out on him* (being cast into the lake of fire, Rev. 19:20). *"*

We read in Revelation that there are seven seals, seven trumpets and seven bowls. Although they all happen chronologically within their own sequence, each set overlaps with the others. For instance, at first sight it looks like the first trumpet is not blown until after the seventh seal is opened, Rev. 8:6, but actually it is blown sometime between the breaking of the first and sixth seals. We know this because the opening of the sixth seal causes a great earthquake and sees the return of Jesus, Rev. 6:12-17, and so the trumpets must start before that. The seventh trumpet and the seventh bowl both happen at about the same time as the sixth seal, because they all cause the same series of catastrophic earthquakes in Jerusalem and cities all around the world, Rev. 16:19, and see the return of Jesus, Rev.11:15-19 and Rev. 16:17-21.

As explained, the seven bowls are the last plagues as stated in Rev.15:1, and are therefore all poured out after the sixth trumpet is blown. The sixth bowl releases the spirits to gather the rulers of the whole world to gather for the last great battle of this age at Armageddon, Rev.16:16.

The seventh trumpet is the one Paul referred to in his letter to the Corinthians:

> *"Listen, I tell you a mystery: We will not all sleep, but we*
> *will all be changed —in a flash, in the twinkling of an eye,*

at the last trumpet. For the trumpet will sound, the dead will be raised imperishable, and we will be changed (the believers remaining on the earth are raptured). *"*

(1 Corinthians 15:51-52)

This last trumpet will bring an end to the present age as well as the glorious return of Jesus when the kingdom of this world becomes the Kingdom of our Lord, Rev.11:15-19.

We are given these three simple sequences so those who go through the Great Tribulation can easily identify which stage they are at to further encourage the Church that God remains in overall control. All of these judgments will happen within the last 1,335 days, initiated by the opening of the first seal which allows the abolition of Temple sacrifice. They end with the angels having a well earned rest in heaven after the seventh seal is broken!

"When he opened the seventh seal, there was silence in heaven for about half an hour."

(Revelation 8:1)

Matthew also refers to the same Jesus' return events of Rev. 6:12-14, and says that the sun will be darkened and the moon will not give its light, Matt. 24:29. However, the stars falling from the sky and the earth fleeing from the presence of the Lord do not happen until the end of the Millennium when the judgment seat of God is set up, Rev. 20:11. The events are recorded here and in other parts of the Old Testament in such a way that makes everything appear to happen at the same time, which has given rise to amillennialism i.e. the belief that we are in the 1,000 year reign of Christ now, and there is no gap between these two cataclysmic acts of God. However, further study shows this is not the case. For instance, we are told Satan is bound in the Abyss during the 1,000 years and cannot tempt or mislead any during that time but Paul says "*the ruler of the kingdom of the air* (Satan)", *Eph.2:2*, is very active today in the world. So, we are clearly not in the Millennium now. Just as the Church age was hidden in times past, so the 1,000 years reign of Christ is still not fully explained at this stage.

All these timings and information are given to encourage the Church during the last traumatic years, to reassure her that God is in overall control and that there will be a definite and known maximum end to the Great Tribulation. Within all this turmoil, the Holy Spirit is seeking to save as many as possible before the final removal of all sinful resistance at the return of Jesus:

> *"I saw heaven standing open and there before me was*
> *a white horse, whose rider is called Faithful and True.*
> *With justice he judges and makes war. His eyes are*
> *like blazing fire, and on his head are many crowns.*
> *He has a name written on him that no one knows but*
> *he himself. He is dressed in a robe dipped in blood,*
> *and his name is the Word of God. The armies of*
> *heaven were following him, riding on white horses and*
> *dressed in fine linen, white and clean. Coming out of*
> *his mouth is a sharp sword with which to strike down*
> *the nations. He will rule them with an iron scepter. He*
> *treads the winepress of the fury of the wrath of God*
> *Almighty. On his robe and on his thigh he has this*
> *name written:*

KING OF KINGS AND LORD OF LORDS

(Revelation 19:11-16)

In this present age an individual who receives the new birth in Christ is raised and seated with Him in the heavenly Jerusalem, Heb. 12:22. But on Jesus' return, His throne will be transferred to Jerusalem on earth from where He will rule Israel and the rest of the nations during the Millennium.

As far as the E.U. is concerned, very significantly there has been little prayer initiated by God in the Church to stop this enterprise from growing. The seventh head of the Beast, the revived Unholy Roman Empire, is starting to raise its head and at the right time God will allow Satan to bring the Antichrist, the eighth head, to international power. We may well see Israel join the E.U. as part of an Israeli/Palestinian peace treaty, bringing it once again under the influence of the Roman Empire where Jerusalem becomes an international capital for all religions. This E.U. covering will be a protection from militant Islamists. Judging from the statue in Nebuchadnezzar's vision, Dan. 2, which represents empires that have ruled over the Jewish nation, we are now living in the time of the feet when baked clay is mixed in with the iron – Islam dispersed throughout the revived Roman Empire but with fundamentalists being unable to integrate because of their beliefs.

Even though the E.U. is currently experiencing major economic traumas, the manipulating spirits that drive it will help ensure its survival, drawing in as many countries as possible that were in the original empire, especially Israel, as Jerusalem is the jewel in the crown of Satan's schemes. The

E.U. politicians have not exercised proper fiscal discipline, causing great financial hardship, especially in some areas of the Eurozone. Yet despite this, most want to stay in it. The leaders are saying more and more that they are in the E.U. primarily for political reasons not for economic ones. When we joined the European Economic Community we were told there was no political agenda to form a super-state, but its elder statesmen are now being honest and saying there was a political plan from the start. Deception is a hallmark of Satan – he entraps people by stealth. This desire for unity to avoid another war in Europe is actually being manipulated at a deeper level by the spirits who rule there and who are working towards putting the Antichrist in power in Jerusalem. The problems in the E.U. will eventually produce a situation from which the 10 end-time kingdoms will come, as prophesied in Daniel 7:24-25. Thankfully their reign of terror with the Antichrist will be short-lived.

> *"The ten horns are ten kings who will come from this kingdom. After them another king will arise, different from the earlier ones: he will subdue three kings. He will speak against the Most High and oppress his holy people and try to change the set times and the laws. The holy people will be delivered into his hands for a time, times and half a time. But the court will sit, and his power will be taken away and completely destroyed forever. Then the sovereignty, power and greatness of all the kingdoms under heaven will be handed over to the holy people of the Most High. His kingdom will be an everlasting kingdom, and all rulers will worship and obey him."*
>
> (Daniel 7:24-27)

Here again, we shall have to see how the detail works out.

Events such as Israel joining the E.U. and domination by the Antichrist must be seen in a positive light as steps towards the final salvation of the Jews and the liberation of Jerusalem. God used World War I to remove the Turks from ruling Israel, World War II to begin a major uprooting of Jews in Europe and He will use whatever happens in the future to bring His salvation to the Jewish nation. I believe all these events are points on the long straight line sloping upwards, representing God's restoration of the Jewish nation that He showed me back in 1977.

The Jews have paid dearly for their rebellion over the millennia but since 1948 God is fighting for them once again. He will not hesitate in bringing extreme pressure to humble them in order that they might willingly receive His salvation. The last years of great trauma will see the Jewish nation fully restored to every part of the land and the nation turning to their Messiah, the Lord Jesus, in full repentance and faith. As Paul wrote:

"And all Israel will be saved"

(Romans 11:26)

After all the events of this age, a wonderful scripture in Isaiah sums up the Lord's overall plans for Jerusalem in the Millennium, where Jesus' throne will be transferred from heaven!

"For Zion's sake I will not keep silent, for Jerusalem's sake I will not remain quiet, till her righteousness shines out like the dawn, her salvation like a blazing torch. The

nations will see your righteousness, and all kings your
glory; you will be called by a new name that the mouth of
the LORD will bestow.

You will be a crown of splendor in the LORD's hand,
a royal diadem in the hand of your God. No longer will
they call you Deserted, or name your land Desolate. But
you will be called Hephzibah, and your land Beulah; for
the LORD will take delight in you, and your land will be
married*. As a young man marries a young woman so will*
your Builder marry you; as a bridegroom rejoices over his
bride, so will your God rejoice over you.

I have posted watchmen on your walls, O Jerusalem:
they will never be silent day or night. You who call on the
Lord, give the Lord no rest till he establishes Jerusalem
and makes her the praise of the earth (hence the growing
worldwide desire in the Body of Christ to pray for Israel).
The Lord has sworn by his mighty right hand and by his
mighty arm: ***Never again will I give your grain as food***
for your enemies *... for which you have toiled; but those*
who have harvested it will eat it and praise the Lord ...
Say to the Daughter of Zion, "see your Saviour comes!""

(Isaiah 62:1-9 and 11)

What a glorious destiny!

Replacement Theology spiritualises the whole passage
by saying that because the Church has come to heavenly
Mount Zion, Heb. 12:22-29, God has discarded earthly
Jerusalem. However, Scripture teaches us that this is only a
half truth as God is also in the process of bringing a physical
restoration to the Jewish nation. We are already seeing the
Jews transforming the land with farms and cities – *"the*

wilderness will rejoice and blossom", *Is. 35:1*. In the above passage, Israel's enemies who have occupied the land are said to be eating the Jews' grain. This cannot mean spiritual grain as unbelievers cannot eat the spiritual food of the believer, which is the Word of God! Therefore, it must refer to physical grain in physical Israel.

A rather odd notion to our western mind is that the Lord describes the land as "married", which means He is just as committed to it as to the descendants of Abraham. It is inseparable from Him.

The Lord wants the Church to fully understand these things and has placed us as watchmen on the walls of Jerusalem to pray for the nation of Israel. As well as being able to explain the wonderful good news of Christ to the lost, I believe God also wants us to know what is happening in the world today and why. Much of the Church still needs to repent of an anti-Semitic spirit towards the Jewish nation as well.

I trust this study has simplified and clarified a very complicated subject and helped you to see through the current confusion. The necessity of grasping what the scriptures teach on Israel cannot be underestimated and one of the keys is to see there are two Israels of God in the Bible. God is committed to both. Firstly to the whole nation of Israel because of His calling and promises made to the Patriarchs and their natural seed, which are irrevocable. Then to those Jews and Gentiles who have responded to His call – the second *"Israel of God"*, the only part of the Jewish nation which is saved and through whom the outstanding promises can be fulfilled. Because of the perfect faithfulness of God *"the zeal of the Lord Almighty will accomplish it"*, *Isaiah 9:7*.

But we all need to earnestly seek God as to how we should pray for Israel to work with Him to accomplish this wonderful plan of salvation.

Amen

We hope you enjoyed reading this
New Wine book.
For details of other New Wine books
and a wide range of titles from other
Word and Spirit publishers visit our website:
www.newwineministries.co.uk
or email us at newwine@xalt.co.uk